THE SECOND SET

For Keith and Mary Alice Hoover,
and for my family in Singapore.

S.F.

In memory of Danny Barker.

Y.K.

THE SECOND SET

*The Jazz Poetry Anthology,
Volume 2*

EDITED BY

Sascha Feinstein & Yusef Komunyakaa

Indiana University Press
BLOOMINGTON • INDIANAPOLIS

The paper used in this publication
meets the minimum requirements
of American National Standard for
Information Sciences—Permanence
of Paper for Printed Library
Materials, ANSI Z39.48-1984.

⊚ ™

Manufactured in the United States
of America

**Library of Congress
Cataloging-in-Publication Data**
The second set : The jazz poetry anthology,
volume 2 / edited by Sascha Feinstein &
Yusef Komunyakaa.
        p.   cm.
Includes bibliographical references (p.   ).
ISBN 0-253-33053-X (cl : alk. paper). —
ISBN 0-253-21068-2 (pa : alk. paper)
1. Jazz—Poetry.   2. American poetry—20th
century.   3. American poetry—Afro-American
authors.   I. Feinstein, Sascha, date.
II. Komunyakaa, Yusef.   III. Jazz poetry
anthology.
PS594.J34S43   1996
811'.5080357—dc20   95-53294

1   2   3   4   5   01   00   99   98   97   96

Contents

Preface

The language of music is sort of a motivic language. It's a developmental language in a sense, and there . . . [are] just so many subtle ways that it's used in relationship to the form or the phrase or the period or whatever. I would say that I have worked hardest on my music to develop that kind of language.
   —Bill Evans

The language metaphors adopted by jazz artists to describe their conceptions convey more than the notion that, within the bounds of their unique language system, "musical ideas" should have substance. They also suggest that, for improvisers, the patterns are not ends in themselves, but have ongoing implications for thought.
   —Paul Berliner

The concept of jazz as a language not only evokes analogies between musical and linguistic structures but also the idea that instruments can, in fact, speak to us. Berliner's *Thinking in Jazz*, a provocative and expansive book, discusses at length the ability that jazz musicians have to create a universal language from improvised musical lines. As an example, he addresses the bassist Charles Mingus and saxophonist Eric Dolphy, how they "carry on a musical dialogue in their classic recordings of 'What Love'" with such distinct phrasing "that the listener can almost follow their arguments literally." Berliner's statement explains why in jazz clubs you hear people call out, "Talk to me!" or say, "This music speaks to me." In addition to the pulse of jazz, they hear cadences and inflections that correspond to words, sentences, whole stories.

But if jazz strives to attain the syntactic logic of what Evans calls "a developmental language" of its own, then poetry, without question, strives that much harder to achieve the emotional complexity and rhythmic drive of music. For seventy-five years, poets have listened to jazz and assimilated certain relationships between the two arts—not merely the issue of language but also the connection between jazz improvisations and poetic narratives as journeys. (This is why Fats Waller once said that each solo should tell a story.) In almost all cases, poems responding to jazz do not offer lyrics or even translations of the sound, but they all respond to this musical language, and the poetry ranges from portraits of jazz musicians to rhythmic abstractions. In conjunction with *The Jazz Poetry Anthology* (1991), this book presents a selection of jazz poems that, we hope, will offer "ongoing implications for thought."

The Jazz Poetry Anthology included many jazz poems that have been heavily anthologized and have therefore become very well known. These poems include Langston Hughes's "The Weary Blues," Frank O'Hara's "The Day Lady Died," Paul Blackburn's "Listening to Sonny Rollins at the Five-Spot," Amiri Baraka's "AM/TRAK," and Michael S. Harper's "Dear John, Dear Coltrane." In contrast, *The Second Set* may initially seem less predictable in its contents, but in fact this second book anthologizes quite a number of poets who might be considered obvious omissions from the first collection: Gwendolyn Brooks, Arthur Brown, Diane di Prima, Henry Dumas, Nikki Giovanni, David Henderson, Anselm Hollo, Haki Madhubuti, Michael McClure, Larry Neal, Dudley Randall, Eugene B. Redmond, Carolyn M. Rodgers, Ntozake Shange, A. B. Spellman, Jay Wright, and many others.

The Second Set also fills some of the inevitable gaps with regard to the history of jazz poetry, particularly poems written before World War II as well as those from the Black Arts Movement of the 1960s. Like the first anthology, it also comprises several of the strongest contemporary writers from a range of cultural backgrounds, including Ai, Rita Dove, Martín Espada, Joy Harjo, Keorapetse Kgositsile, Michael Longley, Mwatabu Okantah, Charles Simic, Lorenzo Thomas, Derek Walcott, Ron Welburn, and Yevgeny Yevtushenko. In short, *The Second Set* embraces a wide variety of poems informed by jazz, and this ensemble of poetry, coupled with many statements of poetics, will inspire, we hope, engaging discussions on the nature of jazz poetry.

One of the difficult editorial decisions concerned the selection of pre–World War II poetry; apart from the work by Langston Hughes, Sterling A. Brown, and Melvin B. Tolson (all of whom appeared prominently in *The Jazz Poetry Anthology*), most of the poems from that period lacked substantive achievement, despite historical fascination. It was tempting, for example, to anthologize the racist "Jazz Cannibal" (published anonymously in *Punch* magazine in 1924 and in the *Literary Digest* in 1925), or other poems, such as "Jazz" by Arthur Guiterman and "Jazz Dance" by Amy Lowell, which evoke the general discomfort with or condescension toward jazz in the early twentieth century. Of similar interest were those poems of the early 1940s—including Ethel Jacobson's "Air de Barrelhouse" and Anderson Scruggs's "Meditations on Swing"—that continued the racist propaganda about jazz. There were also entire collections that focused exclusively on jazz-related verse, such as Clement Wood's *Greenwich Village Blues* (1926) and Maxwell Bodenheim's *Bringing Jazz!* (1930). But in all these instances and many others, the poetry itself had limited musicality. We have chosen poems by Hart Crane, e. e. cummings, DuBose Heyward, Vachel Lindsay, and Muriel Rukeyser because of their literary presence in the poetry circles of the time. We also selected a representative poem by Frank Marshall Davis as a brief introduction to his sincere and more-successful ventures into jazz-related literature, as well as a somewhat obscure but interesting poem by Ernst Moerman ("Louis Armstrong," collected in Nancy Cunard's 1934 anthology, *Negro*) as translated by Samuel Beckett.

Many of the poets in both anthologies have written extensively about jazz, so much so that jazz seems to have influenced their work as much as literary sources. Sometimes poems have been written as a series, which might be seen as being parallel to jazz musicians who improvise several choruses. Some poems in this collection, in fact, have been selected specifically to be read either as a series or as a group of reflections on the same subject, such as Alvin Aubert's poems in tribute to Bessie Smith, Thulani N. Davis's poems on Cecil Taylor, a trio of Monk poems by Dave Etter, two sections from Doughtry "Doc" Long's *Black Love Black Hope*, Sandra McPherson's poems in honor of Junior Wells, three pieces by James Cushing (all titled after jazz standards), and blues poems by Raymond R. Patterson and Barry Wallenstein.

In the late 1960s and early 1970s, two presses from Detroit, Broadside and Lotus, published a great deal of jazz poetry, and we have tried to represent poets published both by Broadside (Alvin Aubert, Gwendolyn Brooks, Lance Jeffers, Keorapetse Kgositsile, Doughtry "Doc" Long, Haki Madhubuti, Dudley Randall) and Lotus (Samuel Allen, Houston A. Baker, Jr., James A. Emanuel, Oliver LaGrone, Naomi Long Madgett, Ron Welburn). The poetry by some of these writers has not been reprinted nearly enough in recent years; this book, like *The Jazz Poetry Anthology*, presents work not only by mainstream figures, such as John Berryman and Richard Hugo, but also by young poets and others who have been, for one reason or another, marginalized by popular academic anthologies.

Inevitably, certain monumental jazz musicians (such as John Coltrane, Thelonious Monk, Charlie Parker) have had a profound influence on poets. The Music Appendix indicates certain imbalances, but we have also made an effort to include poems that are tributes to or were inspired by famous players not often addressed in poetry: Gil Evans (Ron Overton), Ella Fitzgerald (Carolyn M. Rodgers), Curtis Fuller and Booker Little (Rick Madigan), Jimmy Guiffre (Thomas McGrath), Jim Hall (Adrian Mitchell), Hank Mobley (Cornelius Eady), Art Pepper (Edward Hirsch, David Meltzer), Woody Shaw (Michael Castro), Sun Ra (David Jauss, Askia Muhammad Touré), and Jack Teagarden (James McKean).

In addition, we have collected several elegies for Chet Baker, including Ai's "Archangel," Mark Doty's "Almost Blue," and Miller Williams's "The Death of Chet Baker." In Lynda Hull's "Lost Fugue for Chet," the speaker travels along Amsterdam's canals, passing stone bridges, tarnished doors, a litter of syringes,

Michelangelo boys, cavernous brown cafés. The mysterious setting clouds into images of Baker, who also travels through "chiaroscuroed" landscapes of heroin and jazz. "Lost Fugue for Chet" reads like a series of connected journeys, all inspired by and rooted in the sounds of jazz. Here, and in many other poems, we experience the language of jazz, where a steady pulse—like "a phrase end-lessly/complicated as that twilit dive through smoke"—miraculously fuses the tenderness of April's white blossoms with the city's relentless urban intensity. In that spirit, we hope the two anthologies grouped together will allow for a more comprehensive text with which to explore the history of jazz poetry.

THE SECOND SET

AI

Archangel

for Chet Baker

You stepped through
the Van Gogh blue curtain
into my dream.
That day in Paris,
we sat at the outdoor café for hours.
I had high breasts
and my dress was cut low.
You leaned close to me, so close;
yet, did not touch.
"I don't need to," you said, "it's the dope,
it's the rush
so much better than lust.
Hush, take a deep breath
and you'll just go to sleep like I did."
I knew you were hustling me,
that underneath the hipster philosophy
lay the same old Chet out to score.
Still, I lent you money, still I followed you
to the pissoir,
where Lucien gave you "le fix."
Shaking his head, he pocketed the money and said,
"I heard you were dead,"
and you answered, "I am."
You said when you slammed into the pavement,
Amsterdam shook, then settled back into apathy,
the way we all do, when we are through
with the foolishness of living.
You ended up sharing your works with a whore
who waited outside the pissoir door,
your generosity as pathetic
as it was predictable.
You wanted sainthood like everybody else.
Instead, you earned the wings
that were too late to save you,

1

but not too late to raise you
up to junkie heaven.
Later, we stood on the steps of Notre Dame.
You were calm, as you pointed to the bell tower.
You said you saw Quasimodo up there,
holding Esmeralda over the edge
by her hair,
but all I saw staring down were the gargoyles
who'd found peace,
because it meant nothing to them.
"I see," I lied, to please you,
but you knew and you blew me a kiss.
You wished me "bonne chance,"
then you eased into flight,
as the cool, jazzy, starry night
opened its arms to retrieve you.

The Man with the Saxophone

New York. Five A.M.
The sidewalks empty.
Only the steam
pouring from the manhole covers seems alive,
as I amble from shop window to shop window,
sometimes stopping to stare, sometimes not.
Last week's snow is brittle now
and unrecognizable as the soft, white hair
that bearded the face of the city.
I head farther down Fifth Avenue
toward the thirties,
my mind empty
like the Buddhists tell you is possible
if only you don't try.
If only I could
turn myself into a bird
like the shaman I was meant to be,
but I can't,
I'm earthbound
and solitude is my companion,
the only one you can count on.
Don't, don't try to tell me otherwise.

I've had it all and lost it
and I never want it back,
only give me this morning to keep,
the city asleep
and there on the corner of Thirty-fourth and Fifth,
the man with the saxophone,
his fingerless gloves caked with grime,
his face also,
the layers of clothes welded to his skin.
I set down my case,
he steps backward
to let me know I'm welcome,
and we stand a few minutes
in the silence so complete
I think I must be somewhere else, not here,
not in this city, this heartland of pure noise.
Then he puts the sax to his lips again
and I raise mine.
I suck the air up from my diaphragm
and bend over into the cold, golden reed,
waiting for the notes to come,
and when they do,
for that one moment,
I'm the unencumbered bird of my imagination,
rising only to fall back
toward concrete,
each note a black flower,
opening, mercifully opening
into the unforgiving new day.

SAMUEL ALLEN

I Say, Mr. A

When
At the close of war
Louis Armstrong returned to the continent
The gentlemen of the press crowded about
Inquiring,

I say, Mr. Armstrong
Which reception did you feel was wah-mah
That before the wa-ah
　　or this?

And Mr. Armstrong replied to the gentlemen,
Saying,

　　I didn't have no thuh-moma-tah
　　but they was both a bitch!

BARON JAMES ASHANTI

Just Another Gig

for Charlie Parker

Rampaging spectral images
darkling strange & imminent
marathon fingers vamping
base chords while 16th note diatribe
focuses like needling rain
trips but never falls
the melody is troublesome
cross-fire of musical notes
running changes from needle's ambrosia
quick-fix for demi-god gypsy flight
on main-line rhythms / be-bop liturgy
with Bird on point
when passion be trial by ordeal
feeding on vanity of the riff

under spotlight constellations
cutting session be like corner fight
with Prussian blue straight razors
urban tragedy of feeling too much
becomes inimitable art
in this civet smelling nocturnal world
audiences set on edge
by stubborn beauty of pain

and here
incompetence be the only enemy /

Hunched shoulders as venue
for monster probe
millennium journey of nights on
tracks in arms
be map of terrible country
whistle-stop tours
endless roll call of nameless dives
road song which tempts with perdition's justice
when immortality be flagrant as pungent sex

on & on
tension ramrod strict
where he is always here
just beyond reach &
brilliance just another
walk-on role /

Legend of the alto's bell
shooting star across life's brocaded tapestry
and cigarette smoke clouds
soar in wild geese formation
when the moon flat-lines midnight skies
something sad illuminates our memory
as we grieve his absence;

rogue cunning stalking future shock
the void a step into the unknown !

ALVIN AUBERT

Bessie

my Gloriana
My Bessie
Bessie Smith,
Enable me.
But first forgive.
Forgive my late arrival.

Forgive this late late rose.
Forgive the lazar place
That would not let you in.
Bessie, forgive my sin.
Forgive the chariot
That would not swing your way.
Forgive Mississippi, Bessie,
Forgive Mound Bayou, U. S. A.
Forgive.
And serve me,
Bessie, in this time
Of our most common need.

Bessie Smith's Funeral

The brief procession.
The crude gray church that pegs the bend
Of a river. After brisk december air

Smoke-white walls,
An artless trim of brown,
Windows unadorned
Except for what of fields beyond
The eye can trace on dusty panes.

Chafed by fiery oration
That rains on salamandered ears,
Naked bulbs retreat
From slaking so much darkness, turn
To dalliance with lilies and a casket
Textured to the dime-store toy that reins
The impish hands of a child close by.

Spirits are abroad in the splintery pews,
Restless in the drafty aisles, will not
Give way to order of service, to such
Superfluous mourning;

One, a burly chantress with a song,
Balks the yokeless choir that grates
The lily-scented air;
Her song is news, begins the dispensation
Of the blues.

HOUSTON A. BAKER, JR.

Tobacco Warehouse Blues

The bluesman in pungent mood,
Has a parallax of shining rails in mind,
When he shouts of riding the blinds,
In the warehouse's second story,
One tale of fields / the other of this moment's song,
Escape from gang labor and long ride beneath the whale's belly,
A prophetic moment as plants took life,
And he and his guitar "up" from Georgie,
Made black men's sore evenings lighter.

The pungent mood of drying leaves rising,
Bob's banging rhythms are sounds of a free man,
A freight-train rider — a mean primer and curer
Of men.

Of Walter White's Father in the Rain

Horrified when they realized their
patient's race, the medical staff
promptly ceased its labors and sent
Walter White's father bumping across the
street in driving rain to the dilapidated
building reserved for Afro-Americans.
 —from *When Harlem Was in Vogue*

Denied,
Like Bessie,
Bleeding in southern rain,
You felt your body jolted
Above gurney wheels,
Water driving into your
Pain-filled eyes.
Your bones shattered by
The physician's speeding car
Cried for mercy,
Some balm to still the agony,

7

And hazily you recall
First moments in the
White wards:
Soft faces of concern
And antiseptic efficiency;
Monitors' quiet beeping;
Now, like Bessie on back roads dying,
You are discovered a son of Ham,
A son-in-law's dark inquiry set the staff humming:

"God-damned **Nigger** . . . My God!"

You feel your crushed body jolted,
Rolling through rain to a colored hospital's
Crumbling wards of rats and decay.
You will pass before day is done.

Evening etches your sons' future,
With Southern rain drops in acid detail,
Rehearses a blues melody of the Empress dying.
Passing in the rain, separate,
And forever unequalled.

DOROTHY BARRESI

Venice Beach: Brief Song

Maybe Zizi is right.
Rocket a mile up, look back,

and we're all just earthlings in restaurants
talking low, trying to figure

one thing out, or
stop one thing from happening.

And all the crystal meth in the world
cannot lift even one of our bodies

free of this argument, or set us clear
of the boardwalk's great

stake in pleasure. Still
the hypodermic shadow of the Capitol Records Building

is oddly comforting,
and the Sufi on rollerskates

promises the next tune is ours
on a boom box he's hoisted

like huge hope to his many-robed shoulder:
Bix Beiderbecke and the boys,

"I'm Coming Virginia."
This is not the life we requisitioned for.

But what can we do now that we're here?
When Larry leaves, when Frances

makes her final point and leaves,
and Zizi never showed (she had something to frame),

I know what I'll do.
Contrive a window like this one

where I'll lean out in the old, theatrical
self-wounding way—oh the buoy bells

of loneliness! Oh the black
candles under waves!—but still

tasting cooler air on my face
like a fire hydrant blowing.

Like a different promise.
Then I'll bless the heads of the insane skateboarders,

those little dooms in their
acid-orange knee pads.

Last night they kept me awake
with their breakneck wheels, their passion. Tonight

I'll watch them marry the pit
city fathers laid years ago, and imagining that

gesture of local
wisdom or submission

will be like imagining this prayer for a change:
to be truly blonde, and just once

blown away, flying and flying and flying.

PAUL BEATTY

Sitting on Other People's Cars

this mingus CD
reminds you of me

our friendship workshop
where nat hentoffian gizzard driven
record jacket criticism rhythms
trickled from the starsky n hutch spinout swirl

                              in the crown of yo head
                    ran down
                    your back
          with the bumpidy syncopation

               of a bestfriends knuckle
          rubbin up and down your spine

till some drummers high hat tapped
the side of your neck

did you get the chills
                         yeah kinda

twenty some odd years old
and i wanted to call your mother

          ask her
          if you could spend the night
          writing on my back

could never tell the difference between
a small kay and an h

               well sometimes i could tell
                 i would just say i couldnt
                    so you would have to write it again

our compositions
                    were secret missions
                    me on flashlight
                              you on bow n arrow

10

and the apple jack sweetened milk
completed the triptych riffs
that kissed us off

into our solo careers   and   the reverb of the mingus years
that im just now hearin   still give me the chills

JOHN BERRYMAN

Dream Song 68

I heard, could be, a Hey there from the wing,
and I went on: Miss Bessie soundin good
that one, that night of all,
I feelin fair mysef, taxes & things
seem to be back in line, like everybody should
and nobody in the snow on call

so, as I say, the house is givin hell
to *Yellow Dog*, I blowin like it too
and Bessie always do
when she make a very big sound—after, well,
no sound—I see she totterin—I cross which stage
even at Henry's age

in 2-3 seconds: then we wait and see.
I hear strange horns, Pinetop he hit some chords,
Charlie start *Empty Bed*,
they all come hangin Christmas on some tree
after trees thrown out—sick-house's white birds',
black to the birds instead.

GWENDOLYN BROOKS

Queen of the Blues

MAME was singing
At the Midnight Club.
And the place was red

11

With blues.
She could shake her body
Across the floor.
For what did she have
To lose?

She put her mama
Under the ground
Two years ago.
(Was it three?)
She covered that grave
With roses and tears.
(A handsome thing
To see.)

She didn't have any
Legal pa
To glare at her,
To shame
Her off the floor
Of the Midnight Club.
Poor Mame.

She didn't have any
Big brother
To shout
"No sister of mine ! . ."
She didn't have any
Small brother
To think she was everything
Fine.

She didn't have any
Baby girl
With velvet
Pop-open eyes.
She didn't have any
Sonny boy
To tell sweet
Sonny boy lies.

"Show me a man
What will love me
Till I die.

Now show me a man
What will love me
Till I die.
Can't find no such a man
No matter how hard
You try.
Go 'long, baby.
Ain't a true man left
In Chi.

"I loved my daddy.
But what did my daddy
Do?
I loved my daddy.
But what did my daddy
Do?
Found him a brown-skin chicken
What's gonna be
Black and blue.

"I was good to my daddy.
Gave him all my dough.
I say, I was good to my daddy.
I gave him all of my dough.
Scrubbed hard in them white folks'
Kitchens
Till my knees was rusty
And so'."

The M.C. hollered,
"Queen of the blues!
Folks, this is strictly
The queen of the blues!"
She snapped her fingers.
She rolled her hips.
What did she have
To lose?

But a thought ran through her
Like a fire.
"Men don't tip their
Hats to me.
They pinch my arms

And they slap my thighs.
But when has a man
Tipped his hat to me?"

Queen of the blues!
Queen of the blues!
Strictly, strictly,
The queen of the blues!

Men are low down
Dirty and mean.
Why don't they tip
Their hats to a queen?

The Sundays of Satin-Legs Smith

INAMORATAS, with an approbation,
Bestowed his title. Blessed his inclination.

He wakes, unwinds, elaborately: a cat
Tawny, reluctant, royal. He is fat
And fine this morning. Definite. Reimbursed.

He waits a moment, he designs his reign,
That no performance may be plain or vain.
Then rises in a clear delirium.

He sheds, with his pajamas, shabby days.
And his desertedness, his intricate fear, the
Postponed resentments and the prim precautions.

Now, at his bath, would you deny him lavender
Or take away the power of his pine?
What smelly substitute, heady as wine,
Would you provide? life must be aromatic.
There must be scent, somehow there must be some.
Would you have flowers in his life? suggest
Asters? a Really Good geranium?
A white carnation? would you prescribe a Show
With the cold lilies, formal chrysanthemum
Magnificence, poinsettias, and emphatic
Red of prize roses? might his happiest
Alternative (you muse) be, after all,
A bit of gentle garden in the best

Of taste and straight tradition? Maybe so.
But you forget, or did you ever know,
His heritage of cabbage and pigtails,
Old intimacy with alleys, garbage pails,
Down in the deep (but always beautiful) South
Where roses blush their blithest (it is said)
And sweet magnolias put Chanel to shame.

No! He has not a flower to his name.
Except a feather one, for his lapel.
Apart from that, if he should think of flowers
It is in terms of dandelions or death.
Ah, there is little hope. You might as well—
Unless you care to set the world a-boil
And do a lot of equalizing things,
Remove a little ermine, say, from kings,
Shake hands with paupers and appoint them men,
For instance—certainly you might as well
Leave him his lotion, lavender and oil.

Let us proceed. Let us inspect, together
With his meticulous and serious love,
The innards of this closet. Which is a vault
Whose glory is not diamonds, not pearls,
Not silver plate with just enough dull shine.
But wonder-suits in yellow and in wine,
Sarcastic green and zebra-striped cobalt.
All drapes. With shoulder padding that is wide
And cocky and determined as his pride;
Ballooning pants that taper off to ends
Scheduled to choke precisely.
                                            Here are hats
Like bright umbrellas; and hysterical ties
Like narrow banners for some gathering war.

People are so in need, in need of help.
People want so much that they do not know.

Below the tinkling trade of little coins
The gold impulse not possible to show
Or spend. Promise piled over and betrayed.

These kneaded limbs receive the kiss of silk.
Then they receive the brave and beautiful
Embrace of some of that equivocal wool.

15

He looks into his mirror, loves himself—
The neat curve here; the angularity
That is appropriate at just its place;
The technique of a variegated grace.

Here is all his sculpture and his art
And all his architectural design.
Perhaps you would prefer to this a fine
Value of marble, complicated stone.
Would have him think with horror of baroque,
Rococo. You forget and you forget.

He dances down the hotel steps that keep
Remnants of last night's high life and distress.
As spat-out purchased kisses and spilled beer.
He swallows sunshine with a secret yelp.
Passes to coffee and a roll or two.
Has breakfasted.

              Out. Sounds about him smear,
Become a unit. He hears and does not hear
The alarm clock meddling in somebody's sleep;
Children's governed Sunday happiness;
The dry tone of a plane; a woman's oath;
Consumption's spiritless expectoration;
An indignant robin's resolute donation
Pinching a track through apathy and din;
Restaurant vendors weeping; and the L
That comes on like a slightly horrible thought.

Pictures, too, as usual, are blurred.
He sees and does not see the broken windows
Hiding their shame with newsprint; little girl
With ribbons decking wornness, little boy
Wearing the trousers with the decentest patch,
To honor Sunday; women on their way
From "service," temperate holiness arranged
Ably on asking faces; men estranged
From music and from wonder and from joy
But far familiar with the guiding awe
Of foodlessness.

           He loiters.

                   Restaurant vendors
Weep, or out of them rolls a restless glee.
The Lonesome Blues, the Long-lost Blues, I Want A
Big Fat Mama. Down these sore avenues

Comes no Saint-Saëns, no piquant elusive Grieg,
And not Tschaikovsky's wayward eloquence
And not the shapely tender drift of Brahms.
But could he love them? Since a man must bring
To music what his mother spanked him for
When he was two: bits of forgotten hate,
Devotion: whether or not his mattress hurts:
The little dream his father humored: the thing
His sister did for money: what he ate
For breakfast—and for dinner twenty years
Ago last autumn: all his skipped desserts.

The pasts of his ancestors lean against
Him. Crowd him. Fog out his identity.
Hundreds of hungers mingle with his own,
Hundreds of voices advise so dexterously
He quite considers his reactions his,
Judges he walks most powerfully alone,
That everything is—simply what it is.

But movie-time approaches, time to boo
The hero's kiss, and boo the heroine
Whose ivory and yellow it is sin
For his eye to eat of. The Mickey Mouse,
However, is for everyone in the house.

Squires his lady to dinner at Joe's Eats.
His lady alters as to leg and eye,
Thickness and height, such minor points as these,
From Sunday to Sunday. But no matter what
Her name or body positively she's
In Queen Lace stockings with ambitious heels
That strain to kiss the calves, and vivid shoes
Frontless and backless, Chinese fingernails,
Earrings, three layers of lipstick, intense hat
Dripping with the most voluble of veils.
Her affable extremes are like sweet bombs
About him, whom no middle grace or good
Could gratify. He had no education
In quiet arts of compromise. He would
Not understand your counsels on control, nor
Thank you for your late trouble.

                                        At Joe's Eats
You get your fish or chicken on meat platters.
With coleslaw, macaroni, candied sweets,

Coffee and apple pie. You go out full.
(The end is—isn't it?—all that really matters.)

     And even and intrepid come
     The tender boots of night to home.

     Her body is like new brown bread
     Under the Woolworth mignonette.
     Her body is a honey bowl
     Whose waiting honey is deep and hot.
     Her body is like summer earth,
     Receptive, soft, and absolute . . .

The Third Sermon on the Warpland

Phoenix

"In Egyptian mythology, a bird which
lived for five hundred years and then
consumed itself in fire, rising re-
newed from the ashes."
    —Webster

The earth is a beautiful place.
Watermirrors and things to be reflected.
Goldenrod across the little lagoon.

The Black Philosopher says
"Our chains are in the keep of the Keeper
in a labeled cabinet
on the second shelf by the cookies,
sonatas, the arabesques . . . .
There's a rattle, sometimes.
You do not hear it who mind only
cookies and crunch them.
You do not hear the remarkable music—'A
Death Song For You Before You Die.'
If you could hear it
you would make music too.
The *black*blues."

    West Madison Street.
In "Jessie's Kitchen"
nobody's eating Jessie's Perfect Food.
Crazy flowers

18

cry up across the sky, spreading
and hissing *This is*
it.

The young men run.

They will not steal Bing Crosby but will steal
Melvin Van Peebles who made Lillie
a thing of Zampoughi a thing of red wiggles and
    trebles
(and I know there are twenty wire stalks sticking
    out of her head
as her underfed haunches jerk jazz.)

A clean riot is not one in which little rioters
long-stomped, long-straddled, BEANLESS
but knowing no Why
go steal in hell
a radio, sit to hear James Brown
and Mingus, Young-Holt, Coleman, John,
    on V.O.N.
and sun themselves in Sin.

However, what
is going on
is going on.

Fire.
That is their way of lighting candles in the
    darkness.
A White Philosopher said
'It is better to light one candle than curse the
    darkness.'
            These candles curse—
inverting the deeps of the darkness.

GUARD HERE, GUNS LOADED.
The young men run.
The children in ritual chatter
scatter upon
their Own and old geography.

The Law comes sirening across the town.

ARTHUR BROWN

The Assassination of Charlie Parker

bird does not live
charles christopher parker is dead
is dead in marbled legends
of a bronze benin faced boy with patch-work horn
      and mamma-made macoute
a jazz-juba muse
watching down lester's hands
from kansas city balconies
tracing with bird's eye feather fingers melodic pantomime
      of syncopated braille
bluing a new cartography of flight
at the ear's horizon's deepest touch

is dead whose soul's-song was dust roads was goat paths
      was brooming from gold coast to stoop-down
      to git-back to guinea to harlem
was shuffle blue-black bottom and whoa back buck up
comin down and lord child now's the time and catch up
and huckle buck a stop and double time kalinda
through the four four and misty
      of tin pan alley
was sugar rum molasses sweet back and back
in lockstep in coffle and in harvest of heart-drought
is dead in chili parlors and cherokee
in the recycled but unresurrected riff
in turn your money green
is dead in the elegant laps of hip debutantes
dead to tommy dorsey's horn-rim
      glasses
to bennygood man and the wrong note
is dead in taxicabs
      nodding to everywhere
out in the out chorus
      and the vamp is dead
      to smack
to smacked back
screeching A Train subway and so soon and bye baby the obscene solo

come shitty come yuk yuk come tee hee come mellow
    fucked up and over
funny phoenix orgasmic out of the asshole of he gone
    is dead
in all the bop visioned and bop spent
    stations of the breath
is dead
    to BE
bop charles christopher parker is yardbird-dead
    o-rooney

Callin Buddy
Bolden

callin buddy   bolden callin
sweet
calls to and fo plumblack
shimmy
hipted congo loves
callin

CALLIN
(tongueless tunes)
big leg woman
why u be so mean
got plenty
hamfat woman
but u cut so lean
big leg woman
why u
cut yo meat so lean

CALLIN
cutta cuttin bolden
dap black buddy bolden
who play new orleans
lousianna blues f real
who say

SHAKE YO ASS
TO THE BRASS

BUDDY BOLDEN WHO TALK BAD
who play f pimps n them
who say

i'm buddy bolden
n i'm king
in lincoln park
its me that come to see
play f happy
play f sad
birth death day
n boogie
in the dark

CALLIN BUDDY BOLDEN
HORN RISING LIKE
A SPECIAL RISING SUN
BUDDY WHOSE NOTES DANCE N
WRING WITH THE YOUNG FINE ONES
LIKE WIND IN THE CANE

man say play clean
lawyers doctors
teachers things
inside

i play f them
dont wonta hide
play f hannah
play f rain

CALLIN BUDDY BOLDEN
CALLIN BUDDY BOLDEN
CALLIN BUDDY BOLDEN
WHO'S GONE INSANE

CHRISTOPHER BUCKLEY

Nostalgia

We will see more passing than any,
carry our fathers' grief
through three cultures.
And he tells me how that time,
highschool to the after-war-years,
runs together like a suit of cards,
Hearts let's say,
with Big Bands, the Big Beat, and Swing . . .
Before the war, after the war,
Saturday afternoons in New Jersey,
a swaying crowd of 10,000
at Frank Daily's Meadowbrook,
the sounds of Glen Miller, Claude Thornhill.

During the war, an airbase in Abadan, Iran—
the one disc of Vaughn Monroe worn to static,
once a month culling the frazzled air
for the British Broadcast—
Tommy Dorsey's slide trombone pure
as moisture steaming off a mirror
in the 120 degree shade, Sinatra & The Pied Pipers
with "Blue Evening" and "Once In A While."
Sundays, he'd skin the Persian Gulf in an A-20,
buzz a down-beat through
the anchored Russian fleet.

By the time I was three
I knew how to stand at the plate,
had seen Red Schoendienst turn the double-play,
and heard Julie London's foggy voice.
Now, hair dull as a Mercury dime,
he tells me I'm lucky
to be 30 and unmarried, meaning
the world lost heart by the 50s—
each man home, bent beneath a shoulder's weight
of family and got serious with dollars;
some devil split an atom
under a football stadium
and there was nothing
you couldn't care about.

He looks to me with the obvious,
"How time flies" or "Where do the years go?"
and examines his hands, fingers spread apart
as if he just made a deck of cards disappear
and can't remember how he did the trick.
He doesn't flip to the game of the week
or the up-dated weekend news, rather,
he stacks albums on the Magnavox—
the re-released recordings of an era
when life was coming to only moderate harm.

Playing for Time

for Gary Young

We're walking down Grant, through Chinatown
for no better reason than the sun's worked
free of summer fog. We have a few days off,
are in love with the bright and frivolous
industries of living, and no one cares
if we eat char shiew and sweet bean cakes
on the street, or browse every Paradise Bazaar
for all the beautiful and useless fiddlesticks
we can afford having more or less made it
as far as our mid-30s.

                  And because we have
few illusions about our place in the world
of letters, we slip into the LI PO, built out
to the sidewalk like a river cave and easily
as dark. We drink fashionable Chinese beer
and hang the expense; there's plum wine,
Three Snake Liquor above the bar, but also
pinball in the back, red plastic lanterns
and local news on the portable TV —
somehow, they knew we were coming . . .

In a minute, our eyes adjust and we discover
the ancient, life-sized painting of the poet
at our backs, glowing in an amber varnish
and the casual patina from smoke — beneath
a bare cherry tree, he accepts a cup of wine,

small honor and greeting for his work;
and despite the poverty of his station,
he is as serene as the thin clouds, content
with the little thing he does — and so we
order another Tsing Tao.

                    And to show that
such illustrious institutions are really
named for poets, we take a photo at the door
before sauntering down the block toward
what sounds like a disc of vintage jazz
some shop's cranked up to draw a crowd —
but it's two men, impromptu on guitar and sax,
wedged in a doorway astride milk crates
playing "Body And Soul" as pure and smooth
as the pink negligee silky in the sax's mouth,

which mutes and mellows, keeps the cops away.
The other fellow fingers a forty buck steel string
as effortlessly as if it were a Les Paul,
as if he'd taught Barney Kessel how to chord.
They lay it down easier than that buttered pearl
of a sun dipping west, and no power like theirs —
sweet as a breeze, cheap as it comes, and we have
to wonder why we're the only ones stopping to drink
it in, to drop a dollar onto the worn fur of the case,
or why Dexter Gordon,

                    who's cool and comfortable
atop Manhattan, is glorious and this guy's not?
They are too fine, steady and full of that
blue river and resolve of jazz to be playing
for drinks; certainly too little in it for dope.
We tell ourselves this must only be the world,
oblivious by turns and late in the afternoon,
and this is nothing if not the best there is —
place to place for supper, for dignity after
a bad job's beaten the daylights out of you.

They slide into Ben Webster's "I Got It Bad
And That Ain't Good" and his tremolo beyond
the last note flutters, his after-riff breathes
the signature of the man inside, yet outside
the evanescent body of the song — that wind-
beat releasing its heart-tight rhythm, phrasing

balanced on the air like clouds on light . . .
they're playing to put something real between
their four good hands, playing for time until
a better world comes along.

MICHAEL CASTRO

Blew It

for Woody Shaw

through the tobacco haze
& the clatter of cocktails
through the stench of spilled beer
& the lurching boilermakers
out of the darkness of the pit
where the vipers of the night entwine
he gave language to the black rose

Yeah, they said, he gave language
to the emptiness they shared
he gave them prayer & they said, *Yeah*

he screeched from the ache in his balls
intricate & instinctive as a spider
his belly blown lines spun a symmetry
spanning the void, flies buzzed quizzically
round his notes on their way to the silent gods
& the chorus echoed *Yeah*
as he quenched their summer thirst

He was troubled, he was troubled
by their trouble, for he took it on
sucked it into the bell of his horn
into his gut where it gnawed & got reborn
made it part of his own storm
& he rained, he rained like a dark cloud
he reigned regal as a pharoah, clean as a queen
o he fluttered like a monarch, like Chuang Tzu,
like a caterpillar waking up & finding out
he can fly

& no one wondered why, they just let him die
they just said, *Yeah,* & let him die

for he gave language to the black rose
& down, down in the dankness where its root grows
the cyclopean train shrieked in the tunnel of the soul
a thousand toilets flushed & the excrement of the city rushed
& gargled through the labyrinthine network of subway pipes
a murderous *shakti* current injected the third rail eye
with a lobotomous blindness he straddled

sinking his feet in the low slow quicksand—
They said *Yeah,* & lashed him to the tracks
O he had to hear that iron Siren's song

When it came hurtling & wailing out of the darkness
he had to sing along
had to embrace that Golgothan face
for it was late & he was headed home
He'd had too much to drink & he couldn't think
He just blew what he knew to be true
giving language to the black rose
raining all over it so it grows

& no one wondered why
they just said *Yeah,* & let him fly

RICHARD CECIL

Richard's Blues

for Ray Charles

At three A.M., alone, not sleepy,
I click on my lamp and prop
a borrowed *Shakespeare* on my chest.
It opens automatically
to an often torn and retaped etching
depicting Shakespeare as he dips
his quill into an earth-shaped inkwell.
On his desk a foolscap sheet's
inscribed ornately with the motto:

27

WHO READS THIS READS THE BOOK OF LIFE
but underneath the etching's frame
someone's defaced the scrollwork label,
changed THE BARD into THE FART.

I grab my throat to choke my laughter
before it penetrates thin walls
and wakes the widow who needs to watch
TV till two before she sleeps,
or lies down bravely in her dark,
as Juliet lies in her tomb,
to wait for sleep or death to come.
While I read through the graveyard scene
of *Romeo & Juliet,*
I think of we who survive our grief
when Juliet sheaths that dagger
into her perfect teenage heart
and leaves me gasping, for at her age

I, too, planned to stab myself
with a kitchen knife I took to bed.
I lay down naked on my sheets
on a steamy night in early August
and squeezed its roughened plastic handle
with my right hand while with my left
I tuned Hotrod's *Rocketship Show*—
all-night blues from Baltimore—
on my transistor radio.
Ray Charles sang "Georgia," "Born to Lose,"
and Little Richard wailed "Lucille"
while I meditated suicide.
As Ray crooned *love, oh careless love,*

I decided to send myself to hell,
not live diminished, loveless life
and die and go to hell years later.
Heaven was a girl who wouldn't have me
because I was the wrong religion,
she said, but I knew other reasons.
I couldn't dance with grace or talk
of anything but sticky feelings.
She must have known I would have turned

Mohammedan for one real kiss;
my soul already was condemned
for sacrilege as well as lust—
sins written plainly on my heart.

I've lived my life in pain, sang Ray,
and I knew what he meant that night.
I gripped the sweaty handle hard
and pointed the knife blade at my chest,
but waited to hear the final song,
which Hotrod huskily announced
was for those unrequited lovers
staying up till dawn with him:
If I could moan like a moaning dove,
how I'd moan for the one I love.
As Ray Charles sang, the sun came up,
driving shadows from my room.
The mourning doves began to sing

in the gutter underneath my window
while a horse cart clip-clopped past our house,
its driver crying *hard crabs*.
I realized that I was hungry,
and when I heard my mother call
from her bedroom window for him to wait,
I dropped the knife and slept till noon . . .
Now sunlight's streaming in *this* room,
and the widow has just tuned in "Morning."
I lay this battered *Shakespeare* down
feeling sad, as I did back then,
but grateful to those geniuses
who wrote and sang their lost high passion.

KAREN CHASE

What You Can't See

In the winter stadium, picturing
what you can't see, Leontyne
Price or Lena Horne, the night
the trumpet player died, people

picnicking on the lawn. For him,
his cohorts broke into some long Bach,
then some jazz, wanting songs
to reflect from the nearby lake.
The players played color tones,
saxophones could have grazed his skin.
Picture blues swinging off this empty stadium.

All night looking
out the train window to Birmingham.
Watching I couldn't see what,
turned the light out, pulled
the bed down, watched
the whole state of Virginia in the dark.

It gets light.
I ask a trainman the name of a low
pink week that grows by the track.
"Honey, we call them daffodils."
There's nothing here universal. Cows
are lounging now in what must be Georgia.
Trees that lost their names last night come
clean this morning, dirt red as blush.

JANE COOPER

Wanda's Blues

Ortega Public School, 1932

Wanda's daddy was a railroadman, she was his little wife.
Ernest's sister had a baby, she was nobody's wife.
Wanda was the name and wandering, wandering was their way of life.

Ernest's sister was thirteen, too old for school anyway.
When Ernest couldn't pass third grade, they kept him there anyway,
hunched up tight in a littler kid's desk with his hair sticking out like hay.

But Wanda was small and clean as a cat, she gave nothing away.

At school the plate lunch cost ten cents, milk was a nickel more.
Shrimps were selling for a nickel a pound — those shrimpers' kids were real
        poor,
they lived in an abandoned army camp, the bus dropped them off at the
        door.

Gossip in the schoolyard had it that Wanda swept and sewed
and cooked the supper for her daddy when he wasn't on the road.
She never told where she ate or she slept, how she did her lessons, if she had
        an ol' lamp. . . .
That wasn't the traveling man's code.

Wanda was smart and watchful, we let her into our games.
Wanda always caught on quick whether it was long division or games.
She never gave a thing away except for her lingering name.

I would say it over: *Wanda   Wanda*

April, and school closed early. We never saw her again.
Her daddy loved an empty freight, he must have lit out again.
Wanda-a-a-a the steam whistle hollered. O my American refrain!

HART CRANE

For the Marriage of Faustus and Helen

[II]

Brazen hypnotics glitter here;
Glee shifts from foot to foot,
Magnetic to their tremolo.
This crashing opéra bouffe,
Blest excursion! this ricochet
From roof to roof—
Know, Olympians, we are breathless
While nigger cupids scour the stars!

A thousand light shrugs balance us
Through snarling hails of melody.
White shadows slip across the floor
Splayed like cards from a loose hand;

31

Rhythmic ellipses lead into canters
Until somewhere a rooster banters.

Greet naïvely—yet intrepidly
New soothings, new amazements
That cornets introduce at every turn—
And you may fall downstairs with me
With perfect grace and equanimity.
Or, plaintively scud past shores
Where, by strange harmonic laws
All relatives, serene and cool,
Sit rocked in patent armchairs.

O, I have known metallic paradises
Where cuckoos clucked to finches
Above the deft catastrophes of drums.
While titters hailed the groans of death
Beneath gyrating awnings I have seen
The incunabula of the divine grotesque.
This music has a reassuring way.

The siren of the springs of guilty song—
Let us take her on the incandescent wax
Striated with nuances, nervosities
That we are heir to: she is still so young,
We cannot frown upon her as she smiles,
Dipping here in this cultivated storm
Among slim skaters of the gardened skies.

STANLEY CROUCH

The Revelation

for John Coltrane

To tremble in prayer and trepidation
To tremble against trepidation in prayer
Screech   Scream   Cry
To tremble in prayer against trepidation
Screech-screech   Holler   Cry   Scream

To tremble with prayer
and arch the muscles of my back
in face of trepidation,
transparent beads bubbling from my forehead
      SCREECH   CRY:
Bird of blood with razor-sharp wings of boiling
stone fallen from God into my throat
claws my tonsils and sticks its feet
way down into my stomach
and I double over trying to vomit
forth this bird
to the rhythms of anklets ashake
in the dance of a black—blue-black
blue-black a black blue-black African Witch Doctor
wailing wailing—
scream high out into God,
fall heavily from the pole
of light He offers to the snow
of doubt that freezes
all Spirits' dancing gallop
to slabs of ice across the tongue:

Father, Father, understand me
Maker, Purification, Psalm of Warmth within Light
understand the reverent screams
of this confused devotee:
My journey like the invisible belt of the equator
that divides the world has been long,
the prongs of pain like an acne of lava
have raised their tips within my heart
I have lain high with the stone hips of Satan
crushing my head, weighing my thoughts
as though magnetized to gigantic boulders
falling in the hot hole of hell,
of wherever all these demons
like oceans of flies buzzed and chased me
stuck to me like flying needles to a pincushion
but I saw
as my eyelids tearing from my face
and flapping away
as bats before
dissolving into Pure Light

the trajectory of Your Footsteps scarring the darkness,
the Most Merciful
Power with the
heavy-feathered
wings of wind
lifting my eyes
and I saw
I saw
I saw:

The scum peel back from the sky
and Your Force swell nature with such a light
that my tears boiled my whole body
and I exploded upward
sizzling the air
as an agony too powerful for this fever blister of flesh!

Up on the Spoon

(about Bird: Charles Christopher Parker)

1
That horn chased me
like a hound
and I hid
in spoons
and I boiled
and my insides
turned black
like the bottom of that
spoon beneath that match:
All the darkness,
coming down off bennies
my knees about to split
my dick shrivelled
and disappearing inside my stomach
as my insides scraped together
like a parody of the belly rub
and my horn sucking out all my sadness

like my veins sucked all that smack crest
out of needles:
                    Them pee pees
plenty of em,
I'd beep my horn and there they'd be:
Nothing sweet anywhere,
just the freakishness of
white women following me from club to club
whispering in corners
about giving up head
while I sipped my ice water
and that water turned into the world
when I was sick
had the jitters, the chills
balled up like a rotten loaf of pawn
tickets I couldn't eat
Me: Blasphemer
Me: Bastard
Me: Vandal tearing apart my flesh
and memory,
lynching my music with the second fiddles of the New York
        Philharmonic
just for fix money,
for another chance to drop a cigarette
on a new suit,
sticking needles full of blindness
into my eyes every day.
WHAT ELSE CAN I TALK ABOUT BUT MY SICKNESS
Stick your foot up my ass, please,
outside a tinsel music hall named
after me:
Birdland, the Valley of the Long Distance Runners.
Now hug me in the corner mama
as the horn case's become too heavy to carry
as the sickle man spoons darkness
from the sky with the crescent of the moon
HUG ME!

        2

But please not here with the coffin rotted,
dirt in what was once my mouth,

and the worms grinding against
my bones like my old worn-out records.
Mama, hug me.
Please tell me I'll get well.

e. e. cummings

god pity me whom(god distinctly has)
the weightless svelte drifting sexual feather
of your shall i say body?follows
truly through a dribbling moan of jazz

whose arched occasional steep youth swallows
curvingly the keenness of my hips;
or,your first twitch of crisp boy flesh dips
my height in a firm fragile stinging weather,

(breathless with sharp necessary lips)kid

female cracksman of the nifty,ruffian-rogue,
laughing body with wise breasts half-grown,
lisping flesh quick to thread the fattish drone
of I Want a Doll,
                            wispish-agile feet with slid
steps parting the tousle of saxophonic brogue.

JAMES CUSHING

Autumn Leaves

The end of summer suggested the way
You picture yourself coming out of the rain,
The way disaster avoids collision with bright colors across
A scrim behind a captured city. With one hand
You conduct air and light, expecting only surprise,
Humor, a main idea. The landscape turns on a distant gull.
Tonight's pianist plays every song we know, breaking them like glass
After dropping on bricktop, catching stars.
He is the smiling man painted on the burning building,
At ease in his favorite armchair. My wife
Points to leaves the size of tablecloths,

Veined as madly as cabbage, breeding from the dead and all
Their muddy history. Trees know about it, and spell us
If we get tired and need to rest. But
Sometimes we are given the grace to know
When we've moved far enough in the forest of birds
And darting insects, heavy footed, feeling for the map.

Every Time We Say Goodbye

No situation presents itself,
No smell of stone or water. Here the snow
Lies covered by weeds, and in the distance lies
The cloud from which I speak to you again
Although I'm scared by the present-tenseness
Of the air around your name. After the end
Of the world, you still seem capable of speech
And motion. No questions, you said, no questions,
But every day something old and neat flies south,
Rain beading its wings like falling stars.
I remember watching you assemble a bouquet.
I remember putting my ear to it,
When alone, in hopes it would answer me, and how
Concerned I was when I found it remained silent.
And all I have tonight are a hundred endings,
Old men creaking in folding metal chairs.

Lover Man

Give it all back, even what you were just handed,
He told me, because only then can the dark magic
Begin. He told me a lot of stuff like that.
His fifty-cigarette voice crawled beach to beach
Without him, stopping to lecture seaweed pods
Or shout away gulls who still come back
To land on him. I never saw his feet clearly before:
They were little doors in the sagas, but now
They're drawers holding samples of the soil I know
He won't be buried in. He grows like the star
On a Christmas tree, nourished by the sleep
Of a child who wandered into the house,
Spoke in a chirp, ate soup with us, curled up
On a bookcase. He's a list of moons.

ROBERT DANA

Elegy for the Duke

Ellington is dead

A-train down from Harlem
Tiger-jawed dashikis flashing down from Harlem

Plum and burgundy and fire

Here
London plays a low-tide blues

Spice of tar
Gulls over brown water

And at the Tate
Turner dissolves us all into pure light

into *Eleanor Rose* and *Argonaut* and *Thames Brittania*

Weather as soul

The world turning over

FRANK MARSHALL DAVIS

Jazz Band

Play that thing, you jazz mad fools!
Boil a skyscraper with a jungle
Dish it to 'em sweet and hot—
Ahhhhhhhhh
Rip it open then sew it up, jazz band!

Thick bass notes from a moon faced drum
Saxophones moan, banjo strings hum
High thin notes from the cornet's throat
Trombone snorting, bass horn snorting
Short tan notes from the piano
And the short tan notes from the piano

Plink plank plunk a plunk
Plink plank plunk a plunk

Chopin gone screwy, Wagner with the blues
Plink plank plunk a plunk
Got a date with Satan — ain't no time to lose
Plink plank plunk a plunk
Strut it in Harlem, let Fifth Avenue shake it slow
Plink plank plunk a plunk
Ain't goin' to heaven nohow —
     crowd up there's too slow . . .
Plink plank plunk a plunk
Plink plank plunk a plunk
Plunk

Do that thing, jazz band!

Whip it to a jelly

Sock it, rock it; heat it, beat it; then fling it at 'em

Let the jazz stuff fall like hail on king and truck driver,
     queen and laundress, lord and laborer, banker and
     bum

Let it fall in London, Moscow, Paris, Hongkong, Cairo,
     Buenos Aires, Chicago, Sydney

Let it rub hard thighs, let it be molten fire in the veins of
     dancers

Make 'em shout a crazy jargon of hot hosannas to a fiddle-
     faced jazz god

Send Dios, Jehovah, Gott, Allah, Buddha past in a high
     stepping cake walk

Do that thing, Jazz band!

Your music's been drinking hard liquor
Got shanghaied and it's fightin' mad
Stripped to the waist feedin' ocean liner bellies
Big burly bibulous brute
Poet hands and bone crusher shoulders —
Black sheep or white?

Hey, Hey!
Pick it, papa!
Twee twa twee twa twa
Step on it, black boy

Do re mi fa sol la ti do
Boomp boomp
Play that thing, you jazz mad fools!

THULANI N. DAVIS

C. T. at the Five Spot

4/15/75 Five Spot, N.Y.C., The Cecil Taylor Unit:
Cecil Taylor, Jimmy Lyons, Andrew Cyrille.

this is not about romance & dream
it's about a terrible command performance of the facts
it commands the form/ commands time & space & air
it breathes of journey/brilliant light journey
up thru the where was & who lived
it works those melodies to their pith/to their pulp
it fists & palms the last dirt roads
of lives that have to wear out before they give up
bury me with music and don't say a word
the only preacher is a poet
the text i have not read
but heard screamin' out of saxophones
i have heard this music
ever since i can remember/ i have heard this music
facing the dinge of spots & twofers
in the night/ music/ in the night/music have i lived
ripple stamp & beat/ ripple peddlin'
stomps taps of feet slick poundin' out
tonal distinctions between/ keys & sticks
between funk & the last love song/he romps in beauty
the player plays/mr. Taylor plays
delicate separate licks of poems
brushes in tones lighter & tighter/closer in space
sweet sassy melodies lean in
givin' in at the knees/where its at
to get that stuff/ sweet sassy melodies
hittin' off fast off the top of the stride
sweet sassy melodies knowin what it takes
to even walk those bottom notes/stomps

on those bottoms yes he's been there he knows
the man struggles/bends the meanness
takes hold the meanness of a ditch beatin
sweet sassy/man you gotta wrestle that joy
dig you heels rapid on hard ground/over & over
straighten your back and grab hold of the blindness
of stars fore you let go
this is not about romance
this is the real stuff
commandin' a state/ of the meanness/of the sweetness
of the time it takes/of the space it needs
of the weight of old air/it breathes
& sees like knives thru the thickness of flesh
& the blindness of our very selves
i have heard this music
ever since i can remember/ i have heard this music

C. T.'s Variation

some springs the mississippi rose up so high
it drowned the sound of singing and escape
that sound of jazz from back
boarded shanties by railroad tracks
visionary women letting pigeons loose
on unsettled skies
was drowned by the quiet ballad of natural disaster
some springs song was sweeter even so
sudden cracks split the sky / for only a second
lighting us in a kind of laughter
as we rolled around quilted histories
extended our arms and cries to the rain
that kept us soft together

some springs the mississippi rose up so high
it drowned the sound of singing and escape
church sisters prayed and rinsed
the brown dinge tinting linens
thanked the trees for breeze
and the greenness sticking to the windows
the sound of jazz from back
boarded shanties by railroad tracks
visionary women letting pigeons loose

on unsettled skies
some springs song was sweeter even so

Rogue & Jar: 4/27/77

the players: David Murray, Hamiet Bluiett,
Chas. 'Bobo' Shaw, Fred Hopkins
poet: Ntozake Shange

the "Iron Man" sat with gone eyes/ a witnessing body
& a bad case of sky high low cold cerebral blues
the lady in orange came lit up with love and night blueness
David came with a gold horn/ a copper suit
& Joann's Green Satin Dress
Fred came to do bizness/Bobo came disguised as the Black Knights
Drum & Bugle Corps
& Hamiet Bluiett came from Lovejoy, Illinois 62059
the truth came down twice & i was caught in the middle
when it catches me i'm tasty & dangerous like one more for the road
it laid me out/ it buried me after it worried me
it put ice to my temples & spewed out steam
it was rough/like playing with crackers in Cairo
like playin hard to get on Cottage Grove
it was rough like making love in wet grass
a heat that leaves a chill of remembrance
when the bottom dropped & the floor sank to the metro
i fell in David's bell/where melody is personal
the drum skin began to sweat burlesque
i heard it plead: please the ghosts/cast the flowers
the poem asked what it is to be a man
it was a rough blues/the truth came down twice
& squeezed me like a lemon/ skinned me
& left a tingle there to taste
after such music there is only the quiet shimmer
the glow of eyes being handed back their sight.

DIANE DI PRIMA

I Ching

for Cecil Taylor

                    :mountain & lake
the breakup
                    of configurations.
all the persian rugs in the world
                    are doing a dance,
or conversely smoke.

outside my window the hoods are shouting
                    about Ty Cobb
on Friday nite it was girls
                    & they were drunk.
But the white car stays the same
                    that they lean against.

Notes on the Art of Memory

for Thelonious Monk

        The stars are a memory system
        for thru them
                    we remember our origin
        Our home is behind the sun
        or a divine wind
                    that fills us
        makes us think so.

43

MARK DOTY

Almost Blue

Chet Baker, 1929–1988

If Hart Crane played trumpet
he'd sound like you, your horn's dark city

miraculous and broken over and over,
scale-shimmered, every harbor-flung hour

and salt-span of cabled longing,
every waterfront, the night-lovers' rendezvous.

This is the entrance
to the city of you, sleep's hellgate,

and two weeks before the casual relinquishment
of your hold—light needling

on the canal's gleaming haze
and the buds blaring like horns—

two weeks before the end, Chet,
and you're playing like anything,

singing *stay little valentine*
stay

and taking so long there are worlds sinking
between the notes, this exhalation

no longer a voice but a rush of air,
brutal, from the tunnels under the river,

the barges' late whistles you only hear
when the traffic's stilled

by snow, a city hushed and
distilled into one rush of breath,

yours, into the microphone
and the ear of that girl

in the leopard-print scarf,
one long kiss begun on the highway

and carried on dangerously,
the Thunderbird veering

on the coast road: glamor
of a perfectly splayed fender,

dazzling lipstick, a little pearl of junk,
some stretch of road breathless

and traveled into . . . Whoever she is
she's the other coast of you,

and just beyond the bridge the city's
long amalgam of ardor and indifference

is lit like a votive
then blown out. Too many rooms unrented

in this residential hotel,
and you don't want to know

why they're making that noise in the hall;
you're going to wake up in any one of the

how many ten thousand
locations of trouble and longing

going out of business forever everything must go
wake up and start wanting.

It's so much better when you don't want:
nothing falls then, nothing lost

but sleep and who wanted that
in the pearl this suspended world is,

in the warm suspension and glaze
of this song everything stays up

almost forever in the long
glide sung into the vein,

one note held almost impossibly
almost blue and the lyric takes so long

to open, a little blood
blooming: *there's no love song   finer*

but how strange the change
from major to minor

everytime
we say goodbye

and you leaning into that warm
haze from the window, Amsterdam,

late afternoon glimmer
a blur of buds

breathing in the lindens
and you let to and why not

RITA DOVE

Canary

for Michael S. Harper

Billie Holiday's burned voice
had as many shadows as lights,
a mournful candelabra against a sleek piano,
the gardenia her signature under that ruined face.

(Now you're cooking, drummer to bass,
magic spoon, magic needle.
Take all day if you have to
with your mirror and your bracelet of song.)

Fact is, the invention of women under siege
has been to sharpen love in the service of myth.

If you can't be free, be a mystery.

HENRY DUMAS

Concentration Camp Blues

I aint jokin people, I aint playin around
Wouldnt jive you people, aint playin around

They got the Indian on the reservation
                    got us in the ghetto town

Like when you down home, tryin to get out
A mule in his stall trying to kick out
You gets to it in the ghetto but you aint got out

Wouldn't jive you people, this a natural fact
They watchin us all people, a natural fact
The man is plannin to put a harness on my back

So get with it people, let's get outa his camp
I aint jokin, I got to get outa his camp
Cause the man is ready to number us all with a rubber stamp

Listen to the Sound of My Horn

Listen to the sound of my horn . . .
                    this note you have longed to hear.
Listen to the sound of my horn, I say,
                    this music you have hummed by ear.

I sound the time to rise for the fields.
I moan the rhythm as the congregation kneels.
                    I am the note of air,
                    the voice of your despair.
I cry long nights for you, my people.
I rise early, pull on my coat of cotton
                    and my shirt of tears
                    and a smile to mask my fears.
I tote water to sun-baked trembling lips,
                    and I sing away the pain
                    oozing from hips lashed by the chain of years.

But now, my people, I have a new song.
Listen America, listen every songless ear:
                    Now the congregation rises,
                    Now a burdened land sings.
                    Now the air breathes fresh.
                    Now the rain fills the buckets.
                    The note makes song.
                    The pain washes away.
                    And my horn of clay airs a long signal motif.

Listen to the sound of my horn, my people,
                    this rhythm of years long past.
Listen to the sound of my horn, I say,
                    Great music and I . . . have come at last!

CORNELIUS EADY

Hank Mobley's

Sorry, Hank.
Found out
The Hard
Way. Back
Of an
Album cover,
Years later,
Browsing in a
Record store. It's
The wrong way
To find out.
The guy who
Wrote the
Notes on
The liner
Was pissed.
It appears
That a lot
Of papers
Decided not
To run an
Obit since
By then you
Were not
Quite
John Coltrane.
So this poem
Could be about
The breaks,
And this poem
Might be about
Fire, or

The lack
Of it,
Or this poem
Could deal
With the also-rans,
—You know,
The joke
About the
Guy who
Invents
1 through 6 Up
Then quits,
Throws up his hands
In desperation,
But it was
Your breath
In my ears
As I stood there,
Dumbly speaking
To whom?

Jazz Dancer

I have a theory about motion.
I have a theory about the air.
I have a theory about main arteries and bass lines.
I have a theory about Friday night,
Just a theory, mind you,
About a dry mouth and certain kinds of thirst
And a once-a-month bulge of money
    in a working pair of pants.

I have a theory about kisses,
The way a woman draws a man across a dance floor
Like a ship approaching a new world.
I have a theory about space
And what's between the space

And an idea about words,
A theory about balance and the alphabet,
A theory concerning electricity and the tendons,
A hunch about long glances from across a ballroom

Even though there's a man on her arm,
Even though there's a woman on his arm

And Fire and the Ocean,
Stars and Earthquakes,
Explosions as sharp as new clothes
    off the rack.
When I leap,

Brushes strike the lip of a cymbal.
When I leap,
A note cuts through glass.
When I leap,

A thick finger dreams on a bass string
And all that sweat,
All that spittle,
All those cigarettes and cheap liquor,

All that lighthearted sass and volcanism,
All that volatile lipstick,
All that

Cleaves the air the way a man and woman
Sweet-talk in a bed.
When I leap,
I briefly see the world as it is
And as it should be

And the street where I grew up,
The saxophones,
Kisses
And mysteries among the houses

And my sister, dressing in front of her mirror,
A secret weapon of sound and motion,
A missionary
In the war against
The obvious.

JAMES A. EMANUEL

Get Up, Blues

Blues
Never climb a hill
Or sit on a roof
In starlight.

Blues
Just bend low
And moan in the street
And shake a borrowed cup.

Blues
Just sit around
Sipping,
Hatching yesterdays.

Get up, Blues.
Fly.
Learn what it means
To be up high.

MARTÍN ESPADA

Majeski Plays the Saxophone

"He killed his parents
and buried them
in the city dump,"
the Treatment Director said,
white-haired keeper
of crazy house folklore
in the file cabinet.

Majeski plays the saxophone
down in mental hospital's
abandoned bowling alley,
devils tattooed on his arms,
headshaking overgrown hair and beard
with the murmur of the trembled horn,

bodyrocking to saxophone's
drugged confession.

Social workers caucused,
doctors conferred:
"We don't know
what's wrong with him,"
said one.
"He's a sociopath,"
said another.
"Plays the goddamn saxophone,"
said another.

And Majeski plays the saxophone,
saxophone like a deaf-mute moaning,
like a fugitive's hoarse breathing,
blues from a radio
at the cemetery, posthumous 78
repeating the town secret.

"He's here for the rest of his life,"
the Treatment Director said,
and had to smile
when he said it.
On the ward,
the guards played poker
and squabbled with the patients
over the TV.

Majeski plays the saxophone,
ballad moist and bitter
as the taste of tongue's blood,
swinging slow welled trachea-hot
and forced out the mouth,
jazz.

Shaking Hands with Mongo

for Mongo Santamaría

Mongo's open hands:
huge soft palms
that drop the hard seeds
of conga with a thump,

shaken by the god of hurricanes,
raining mambo coconuts
that do not split
even when they hit the sidewalk,
rumbling incantation
in the astonished dancehall
of a city in winter,
sweating in a rush of A-train night,
so that Chano Pozo,
maestro of the drumming Yoruba heart,
howling Manteca in a distant coro,
hears Mongo and yes,
begins to bop
a slow knocking bolero of forgiveness
to the nameless man
who shot his life away
for a bag of tecata
in a Harlem bar
forty years ago

Dándole la mano a Mongo

para Mongo Santamaría

Las manos abiertas de Mongo:
palmas enormes y blandas
que dejan caer las duras semillas
de la conga con un retumbao,
sacudidas por el dios de los huracanes,
lloviendo cocos de mambo
que no se rompen
aún cuando se estrellan contra la acera,
cantos resonando
en la sala de baile atónita
de una ciudad invernal,
sudando en un apuro de noche del tren A,
para que Chano Pozo,
maestro del corazón percusivo Yoruba,
aullando Manteca en un coro distante,
oiga a Mongo y sí,
comience un bolero
lentamente percusivo de perdón

para el hombre sin nombre
que le tiró la vida
por una bolsa de tecata
en un bar de Harlem
hace cuarenta años

DAVE ETTER

Monk's Dream

A beautiful man is sleeping under a pine tree.
Gentle hands are wrapped around a golden saxophone.
Sunlight plays across quiet knuckles.

COLTRANE!   COLTRANE!

Stuffy Turkey

I limp along, looking for feathers
and strange tracks left by turkeys.

A tin drum bangs in my hot skull.

The birds blow baritone saxophones.

I have left a wife and a mother
snapping wishbones in the cellar.

O cranberry the sharp gray leaves,
the highways of moss, the dead flowers.

Flags, flags: give me torn flags,
red banners to flog the air with.

I will find a fat turkey to kill.
I will stab him 48, 58, 68 times.

I will cut his stuffy head off
and bury it deep in my tin drum.

The snakes blow soprano saxophones.

Can you hear me above all this jazz?

Well You Needn't

I'll play it and tell you what it is later.
  —Miles Davis

Find Uncle Fred's photograph
in the tan attic trunk.

What kind of town is Ashtabula?

Dust Uncle Fred's photograph
with a clean green Kleenex.

What kind of name is Ashtabula?

Put Uncle Fred's photograph
next the aspidistra.

What kind of fun is Ashtabula?

MARI EVANS

Boss Communication

Wes
cradling his ax
the lover
fingering impossible progressions
persuading the submissive
strings to his warm
touch
        coaxing
            cigarette dangling
                intent
                telling it
                    the way it is with him
        smiling
            a personal ecstasy
                and it becomes

                              tumbling sound
                        spilling
                  kaleido/streaking
                        in its anxious heat

                        Messages
                              spirit pulsed
                                    entering the flow
                                    at just the
                                    moment
                  Wes
                  drags the drooping
                  cigarette
                  sighs and nods like
                                          yeaah . . . .
                        If he knows you
                        heard

SARAH WEBSTER FABIO

For Louis Armstrong, A Ju-Ju

Louis, Louis, Louis, Louis,
You gotta go right now,
Louis, Louis, Louis, Louis,
You gotta go right now.

Go on, my man,
move on up a little higher,
you've blown all the trumpet
that any one man can do on earth.
You've made music, shed mirth;
you've paid dues any way you hump it.
Fortune's a gambler's purse; coins made you buyer.
So, go on, my man, take yo' rest.

        Jazz was yo' art. Jazz was yo' life.
        From waif to world impresario, you winged it,
        befo' there were fets, rockets to the moon,
        you entered the Cosmos on notes blown from yo' horn;
        got yo' SOUL in minor key befo' you were born,
        like a mojo, turned the blues of yo' life into a Black tune,

                              56

yo' self into a thing of beauty and envy, the heavy way
you singed it.
Jazz was art to you. Jazz was life.

> Louis, Louis, Louis, Louis,
> You gotta go right now.
> Saint Louis, Saint Louis,
> You gotta go right now.

Go on, my man,
move on up a little higher.
Yeah, you heard me say say Saint, not Satchmo.
Giant among peers, genius, gentleman
Yo' greatness didn't come 'cause God gave you a generous dental plan;
far more than the teeth in yo' smile was what made you catch so.
Fame's a hungry bitch but you had bread enough to buy her.
So Saint Louis, move on up.

> Jazz was yo' art. Jazz was yo' life.
> Graveled voice, groveling, groping from the day you were born,
> asking no quarters, being man among men;
> taking the lows, the downers, the blues making them hi-life,
> taking weary-hearted Blacks all the way back home,
> back, back to Mother Africa, back where we come from,
> back to the natal cord, the tie broken by Slavery's knife,
> back to Beale St., the Mississippi bottom, New Orleans,
> leathering yo' lips—Satchel mouth, working the voodoo
> of yo' horn.
> Jazz was yo' art. Jazz was yo' life.

> Saint Louis Louis, Saint Louis, Louis
> You gotta go right now.
> Saint Louis Louis, Saint Louis Louis,
> You gotta go right now.

Go on, my man,
take your throne on high,
take your place among the immortal host,
do your thing forever, world without end,
as long as music lives in the memories of men.
You who took earth, life, soul, scarred lips and wind
and blew forth Jazz, as much curse as boast
Scoped music in noise, truth in lie.
Saint Louis keep a movin' on.

Jazz is yo' life. Jazz is yo' art.
Yo' birth turned on the Twentieth Century
Like an age come with the wind, you've gone with the wind,
and in between, you blew and mastered the voice of the wind,
and through your music made the life of mankind a little
more free.
And when Saints go marching in, that trip'd be a bummer,
if Black folk checked it out and you weren't in that number.
HELL ——————
O, Dolly, we gotta know whose calling shots
Dealing out those cards to the haves/have nots.
Jazz is life to you. Jazz is Art.

Louis, Louis, Louis, Louis,
we gotta know right now.
Louis, Louis, Louis, Louis
befo' you go right now.
Saint Louis Louis, Saint Louis Louis
you gotta go right now
Saint Louis, Saint Louis
Go Man, Go right now.
Blow, Man, blow right now.
Blow on out
                    of
                         this
                              world.

SASCHA FEINSTEIN

Christmas Eve

You'd think they'd be with family,
At a party, out of town, but it's Miles,
Monk, Bags, Percy, and Klook
In Van Gelder's New Jersey studio.
Twenty-five years later, I fall for
A woman who has both out-of-print LPs,
Together a collage of tunes
From that gig, two cuts of "The Man I Love"
With a mumbled argument that stops

The first take. We tried so many times
To make out the words, unable to hear
Enough through her speakers, pressing together.
Young love. 1954: my parents
Hadn't met, couldn't imagine
The failure of their first marriages
Or why my mother would turn to painting,
To my father's classes, their attraction
Unspoken. Love came to them the way
Miles punctured the air with notes soft enough
To hold a woman, lines floating somewhere
Between Jackson's vibraharp mellifluous
Against Monk's dissonant chords. Late
December. I won't be born for nine years.
It's the holiday, though dad doesn't know it
Yet, that deadens what's left of the marriage,
Days he won't talk about unless
Memory triggers a joke: What not to say
To a wife, how not to listen when you should.
This is the holiday my mother decides
She won't return to the U.S. until
Divorce papers arrive signed, but comes back
For reasons she doesn't understand,
Facing it. Street lamps on her lost complexion.
And who decided to tint the black-and-white
Cover photo of Miles with eyes closed, horn
And Harmon mute now sickly fluorescent?
No snow in Hackensack, but it's cold and
Monk's pissed 'cause Miles asks him to lay out
During trumpet solos. They have words.
Some in the studio leave for dinner
And don't return, regretting forever
Not hearing live the improvisations
That swelled from angry respect and need.
Across the Hudson, my father attends,
By himself, a party in the Village.
My mom's there also, though she's with the husband
She doesn't want, hangs her head
Until hair hides her face, and my father
Doesn't even see her. I wonder, sometimes,
What he would have said, what she would have heard,
If she could have answered at all and could he

Withstand pockets of silence the way Miles
Did not: the second take of "The Man I Love"
Where impatience and Thelonious' time
Cause the trumpet to enter mid chorus.
Monk hammers the bridge, consumes the space,
Cuts him. It's more volatile than their fight
On the first take where Bags peddletones
The intro, his phrases fracturing
To Monk's mutiny, momentary chaos:
"When you want me to come in, man?" and
"Man, the cat's cuttin' the thing," and
"I don't know when to come in, man," and
"I stopped too, everybody—," then Miles,
"*Shhhhhhhhhhh*," hushes the group, and because
He knows for some reason this is important,
That it's part of what makes the music, turns
To the booth, to Van Gelder nervously
Recording the gig, and says, "Hey Rudy,
Put this on the record—*all* of it."

Sonnets for Stan Gage (1945–1992)

Your hands cracked and calloused in summer, bled
    Every winter. *That's the way it's always been,*
        You said, clutching your fingers in a mottled
White towel. All of your unspoken
    Words—the angular elbows and snapped wrists—
        Resonate in memory like cymbals left
Unstruck, forever anticipating the stick's
    Crash. Dammit Stan. You thought death
        Was some young drummer you could cut, the way
You kept outplaying fate with heroin
    Overdoses, a mugger's four-inch blade
        In your chest which now I can only see in
My mind heaving. The clean linoleum tile.
    A nurse washing her hands. The cold bed rail.

Floodlight shadow. Your shoes are stroking
    The platform's edge. Two hours before the gig—
        The drums HAVE to be intimidating!—

And because you think they're not you take a swig
    Of J. D. from a shiny flask. But they were.
        This was pain: each platinum strike drove nails
Into my head. ("STAN!") I'm still caught there,
    Pressed against the auditorium wall,
        Twitching as warm-up shots detonated
My chest. ("STAN! You've made the clock jump
    Forward!") *Yeah, but did they INTIMIDATE?*
        Sticks on the drum kit rug, you walk to the front
Of the stage, fingers slicing the air,
    Flicking blood across rows of empty chairs.

With young people the heart keeps beating even
    After other organs decay, your mother told me
        In the hours when tubes of pure oxygen
Failed to purify your liver, your kidneys—
    Just days after being admitted, amused,
        Almost, that you'd finally quit smoking. (And what
Hipster wrote, "Drummers and poets are used
    Like ashtrays YES"?) I loved how with cigarettes
        You'd sketch Emily Remler's guitar solos
At Fat Tuesday's, and you wanted every note
    She played. *Can you believe it? Thirty-two!*
        ("Was it a heart attack? Someone wrote—")
No, speedball. Impish smile. *But okay, sure—*
    I mean, you know—EVERYONE dies of heart failure.

I expect to see at dusk your rhythmic
    Figure strutting mainstreet, on the way
        To some "no cake" gig, shades and hair slicked
Clean as your black suit, your grin—*Hey, babe!*—
    And news of a book on the Twenties
        Art scene in Paris. You'll tell me you're sure
I won't believe it. And you'll tell me jazz
    Is just another language for the curve
        In a woman's dress photographed from behind.
And look at this. And look at this. And look
    At this. But right now I can't even define
        What loss feels like. Sycamore leaves. My rake
Scrapes up fallen sticks. I feel my dry skin
    Chafe from the air. My hands are bleeding.

WILLIAM FORD

Of Miles Davis

The pop-out eyes belong to Baldwin
But are sadder, meaner, more direct
In their accusations against us.

The French have given him a medal
And assigned him Picasso's genius.
In the Third World he outsells Bird.

Costumed tonight in a shimmering tent
Of silver, he stands under the spot,
Head crook'd, glasses as dark

As the eyes of Tiresias.
He's blowing a funky put-to-gether
Bouquet of malevolent flowers

From *Bitches Brew* and *Live/Evil*
Still daring all comers to take in
The African off-beats and squeaks,

The electric sub-harmonies and shifts
Midstream, notes without place
Except in Black air only—

As from the Devil hisself—the whole sound
Shaking with a cocaine jumpiness
He says he finally did kick.

And yet, here and there, we hear it,
That muted horn from *Kind of Blue*
Almost as slow, almost that orchidaceous

Blossoming drawn from a sadness
Nameless, we think, but for the music—
With Bird close by and Trane coming on.

NIKKI GIOVANNI

The Genie in the Jar

for Nina Simone

take a note and spin it around spin it around don't
prick your finger
take a note and spin it around
on the Black loom on the Black loom
careful baby
don't prick your finger

take the air and weave the sky
around the Black loom around the Black loom
make the sky sing a Black song sing a blue song
sing my song make the sky sing a Black song
from the Black loom from the Black loom
careful baby
don't prick your finger

take a genie and put her in a jar
put her in a jar
wrap the sky around her
take the genie and put her in a jar
wrap the sky around her
listen to her sing
sing a Black song our Black song
from the Black loom
singing to me
from the Black loom
careful baby
don't prick your finger

MATTHEW GRAHAM

After the War; When Coltrane Only Wanted to Play Dance Tunes

for Larry Levis

The sadness of afternoons was unmistakable.
There was no new way
Of seeing. The woman who left me
Could have returned at any time
Breathless, a strand of dark hair
Caught in the corner
Of her mouth. The dance hall of the Audubon
Still held

Its own particular style
Of forgiveness, as familiar
As the headlines of the old newspapers
Stuffed in the glory holes
Between the stalls of the downstairs toilet.

People kept their distance.
Couples two-stepped in tight circles
Among the pigeons and the dusk
And the dice games of the park.

The boys in the shadows
Were not praying,
But only tying their shoes,
And I moved in my own time,
And listened again for saxophones.

I'm quitting this place soon

Was still the tune
The girls mouthed to the gypsy
Cabs along the avenue.

Memorial for Trane

Yeah, man,
I'll help out
with the
memorial for
Trane.
But, I wonder
how come
a people
who dig life
so much
spend
so much
time
praising the dead?
And I wonder
when
we gon
start honoring
our live heroes?

JOY HARJO

Bird

The moon plays horn, leaning on the shoulder of the dark universe
to the infinite glitter of chance. Tonight I watched Bird kill himself,

larger than real life. I've always had a theory that some of us
are born with nerve endings longer than our bodies. Out to here,

farther than his convoluted scales could reach. Those nights he
played did he climb the stairway of forgetfulness, with his horn,

a woman who is always beautiful to strangers? All poets
understand the final uselessness of words. We are chords to

other chords to other chords, if we're lucky, to melody. The moon
is brighter than anything I can see when I come out of the theater,

than music, than memory of music, or any mere poem. At least
I can dance to "Ornithology" or sweet-talk beside "Charlie's Blues,"

but inside this poem I can't play a horn, hijack a plane to
somewhere where music is the place those nerve endings dangle.

Each rhapsody embodies counterpoint, and pain stuns the woman
in high heels, the man behind the horn, beats the heart.

To survive is sometimes a leap into madness. The fingers of
saints are still hot from miracles, but can they save themselves?

Where is the dimension a god lives who will take Bird home?
I want to see it, I said to the Catalinas, to the Rincons,

to anyone listening in the dark. I said, Let me hear you
by any means: by horn, by fever, by night, even by some poem

attempting flight home.

Healing Animal

for L. N. and Michael Harper

On this day when you have needed to sleep forever,
to forgive the pained animal kneading
                              your throat,
Sleep, your back curled against my belly.
I will make you something to drink,
                              from a cup of frothy stars
from the *somewhere there is the perfect sound*
called up from the best-told stories
                              of benevolent gods,
who have nothing better to do.
                    And I ask you
what bitter words are ruining your soft-skinned village,
because I want to make a poem that will cup
                              the inside of your throat
like the fire in the palm of a healing animal. Like
the way Coltrane knew love in the fluid shape
of a saxophone
                    that could change into the wings of a blue angel.

66

He tasted the bittersweet roots of this crazy world,
and spit them out into the center of our musical
                                        jazzed globe.
Josiah's uncle brought his music
          to the Papago center of the world
                    and music climbed out of his trombone
into the collected heartbeat of his tribe.
They had never heard anything like it,
            but it was the way they had remembered, the way
"Chief" Joe Moore must have known when he sang
                              for the very first time
through the brass-boned monster.
All through the last few nights I have watched you fight for yourself
with the eyes I was warned against opening.
                        You think you are asleep
when you turn off the lights, and we blend into the same
                        hot-skinned sky.
The land called miracle is the daughter you never died for and she
stands at the edge of the bed with her slim hand
                            against your cheek.
Your music is a crystal wall with a thousand mouths, kin to trains and
sounds that haven't yet been invented,
                        and you walk back and forth
through it to know it won't betray you.
And in the last seconds before the breaking light,
when you are nearly broken with the secret antelope
of compassion,
            when the last guardian angel has flown west to the Pacific
to see someone else through their nightly death,
a homefire is slowly kindled in the village of your body.
And the smoke of dawn turns all your worded enemies
into ashes that will never rise.
Mythic cattle graze in your throat, washing it with milk.
And you will sing forever.

Strange Fruit

for Jacqueline Peters

I was out in the early evening, taking a walk in the fields to think about this poem I was writing, or walking to the store for a pack of cigarettes, a pound of bacon. How quickly I smelled evil, then saw the hooded sheets ride up in the not yet darkness, in the dusk carrying the moon, in the dust behind my tracks. Last night there were crosses burning in my dreams, and the day before a black cat stood in the middle of the road with a ghost riding its back. Something knocked on the window at midnight. My lover told me:

Shush, we have too many stories to carry on our backs like houses, we have struggled too long to let the monsters steal our sleep, sleep, go to sleep.

But I never woke up. Dogs have been nipping at my heels since I learned to walk. I was taught to not dance for a rotten supper on the plates of my enemies. My mother taught me well.

I have not been unkind to the dead, nor have I been stingy with the living. I have not been with anyone else's husband, or anyone else's wife. I need a song. I need a cigarette. I want to squeeze my baby's legs, see her turn into a woman just like me. I want to dance under the full moon, or in the early morning on my lover's lap.

See this scar under my arm. It's from tripping over a rope when I was small; I was always a little clumsy. And my long, lean feet like my mother's have known where to take me, to where the sweet things grow. Some grow on trees, and some grow in other places.

But not this tree.

I didn't do anything wrong. I did not steal from your mother. My brother did not take your wife. I did not break into your home, tell you how to live or die. Please. Go away, hooded ghosts from hell on earth. I only want heaven in my baby's arms, my baby's arms. Down the road through the trees I see the kitchen light on and my lover fixing supper, the baby fussing for her milk, waiting for me to come home. The moon hangs from the sky like a swollen fruit.

My feet betray me, dance anyway from this killing tree.

(Jacqueline Peters, a vital writer, activist in her early thirties, was lynched in Lafayette, California, in June 1986. She had been working to start a local NAACP chapter, in response to the lynching of a twenty-three-year-old black man, Timothy Lee, in November 1985, when she was hanged in an olive tree by the Ku Klux Klan.)

MICHAEL S. HARPER

Bandstand

Monk's dissonant hat
willing every change of direction;
all those influences in your head
touching the wrong target—
none of this recorded,
the ears of the kitchen painted black,
all the musicians in common clothes,
dressing for the ancestors.

You learned to appreciate the pews,
the cooling iron,
the cooling board where the bodies,
guns in the recording studios,
became the tuning forks,
meals eaten while running in place
for Mother and Dad
who could dance.

A Narrative of the Life and Times of John Coltrane: Played by Himself

Hamlet, North Carolina

I don't remember train whistles,
or corroding trestles of ice
seeping from the hangband,
vaulting northward in shining triplets,
but the feel of the reed on my tongue
haunts me even now, my incisors
pulled so the pain wouldn't lurk
on "Cousin Mary";

In High Point I stared
at the bus which took us to band
practice on Memorial Day;
I could hardly make out, in the mud,

placemarks, separations of skin
sketched in plates above the rear bumper.

Mama asked, "what's the difference
'tween North and South Carolina,"
a cappella notes of our church choir
doping me into arpeggios,
into *sheets of sound* labeling me
into dissonance.

I never liked the photo taken with
Bird, Miles without sunglasses,
me in profile almost out of exposure;
these were my images of movement;
when I hear the sacred songs,
auras of my mother at the stove,
I play the blues:

what good does it do to complain:
one night I was playing with Bostic,
blacking out, coming alive only to melodies
where I could play my parts:
And then, on a train to Philly,
I sang "Naima" locking the door
without exit no matter what song
I sang; with remonstrations of the ceiling
of that same room I practice in
on my back when too tired to stand,
I broke loose from crystalline habits
I thought would bring me that sound.

SEAN HARVEY

The Mighty Tropicale Orchestra

We gather at the ship's unlit front deck
between sets to smoke and talk. Stars
knot the sky as an aftertaste of pop

music echoes from Reflections
Disco. Our ship is not guided by stars:
they have been discredited. Instead

it follows lines of attraction
known to skim the Earth, accurate enough
to take us wherever we want

to go, and we always choose
the same circular path. Soon we'll descend
into the Blue Lagoon Lounge
to play "Fly Me To The Moon,"
a tune we've played for so long now
our favorite licks simply fall

into accustomed, half-conscious slots
until some jerk decides to play
our solo before us, note

for note, causing us to stumble
and occasionally soar. At ten we
hit the crew bar for more cheap

drinks, where dominoes slap
onto rickety tables, until that one
Nicaraguan guy gets too drunk and begins

his threats. On that note, everyone adjourns
to Reflections, to watch the postmodern
southern belles perform their six

practiced moves, and to ingratiate
ourselves with daughters of bankers
and lawyers. A carpet of light extends

from the disco's porthole
over turbulent water, ink blots
in which a broken child

could read the past, and up
to the gloating moon. Tomorrow the ship
lands in La Guiara again. I'll decide

whether to wind through coastal mountains, drop
into Caracas, or watch the procession
of merchant marines and thieves

in a dock-side bar. But first
Passenger Talent Night, eight hours
of numbness for a few moments of wonder.

JOE HEITHAUS

What a Little Moonlight Can Do

You can see her, hair down, sipping a Coke,
wrapped in the orange and green
afgan she loved. Even as she died
you were embarrassed. An hour out,
though, you know she's in hospital white,
and the family's in some homogeneous room
where you'll find Maureen
in your father's lap, Theresa at the window.

You tell me this in Sleepy Hollow, the place
we'd been trying to get to, her deathbed
amidst shadows of the Headless Horseman
and skinny Ichabod Crane. In this real
little town, Hawthorne's dreams
are a joke to folks stuck in the projects,
where you'd moved when your mother got sick
and your father went blind. Now, not far
from where the Midnight Ride took place
in a cut grass field near an earthen dam,
you recall our own glide in the dark:

the thruway south in that sputtering Mercury
with mud from the mountains on the floor.
An ashtray swollen with your menthol butts.
I drove in silence while you traced
the dash like a river on a map
and hummed tunes I didn't know:
*Say It Isn't So, What a Little
Moonlight Can Do*, songs I learned from
Billie Holiday's LP years after the drive.
A moment of grief in her voice like yours
as you guessed we might not make it.

I didn't know anyone who'd died
and couldn't look at you as you told
how she knew you weren't a virgin
but never pressed. Her smile, her touch,
how she loved old jazz and would
spin in the kitchen to Lady Day

72

humming above Webster's breathy tenor,
as she twirled your sisters around,
their legs loose and lifeless in air.

DAVID HENDERSON

Elvin Jones Gretsch Freak

Coltrane at the Half Note

To Elvin Jones/tub man of the
John Coltrane Quartet.
GRETSCH is outstanding on
his bass drum that faces the
audience at the Half Note,
Spring Street, New York City.

gretsch love
gretsch hate
gretsch mother father fuck
fuck gretsch

                     The Half Note should be
                     a basement cafe like the "A" train
                     Jazz/ drums of gretsch
                     on the fastest and least stopping
                     transportation scene in NYC
                     subways are for gretsch
                     "A" train long as a long city block
                     the tenements of the underground rails
                     west 4th
                     34th   42nd   125th
           farther down in the reverse
                                local at west 4th
waterfront   warehouse   truck / produce   vacant
the half note
           our city fathers keep us on the right track
zones /   ozone
             fumes of tracks   / smokestacks

The Half Note
westside truck exhaust and spent breath
of Holland Tunnel   exhaust   soot darkness jazz

speeding cars   noisy /   noiseless
speeding gretsch   tremulous gretsch
Elvin Jones the man behind the pussy
four men love on a stage
the loud orgy
gretsch trembles and titters

                                     gretsch is love
                                     gretsch is love
                                     gretsch is love

Elvin's drum ensemble the aggressive cunt
the feminine mystique
cymbals tinny clitoris   resounding
lips snares flanked /   encircling
thumping foot drum peter rabbit the fuck   take
this   and take   that
elvin behind the uterus of his sticks
the mad embryo
panting sweat-dripping embryo
misshapen /   hunched
Coltrane sane / cock   the forceps
the fox and the hare
the chase
screaming and thumping
traffic of music on Spring Street
'Trane says to young apprentice Ron Ferral "fill in the solids,
get it while it's hot and comely;   Elvin fucks almost as good
as his Mama."
The Half Note is as packed as   rush hour on 42nd & 8th
"A" train territory
Coltrane is off with a hoot
directed supine
nowhere in generalness
into the din and the death
between   bar and tables   reds silver glass molten mass shout
tobacco fumes across the boardwalk
                (coney island is the "D" train change
                at west 4th if you want it)
Coltrane steps the catwalk
                elvin jones drums gretsch
                gretsch shimmy and shout
elvin drums a 1939 ford
99 pushing miles per hour /   shoving barefoot driver
                in the heats /

Coltrane /   Jones
riffing   face to face
instrument charge
            stools to kneecap
many faceted rhythm structure   to   tomahawk
gretsch rocks n rolls   gretsch rattles
fuck gretsch /
                    we know so well strident drums
                    children singing death songs   / war
                    tenor and soprano   high
tenor soar /   flux of drums   chasing
        keen inviolate   blue
the model "T" ford & air hammer
                    Holland tunnel
                    "Avenue of the Americas"
                    cobbled stones /   din of rubber
                    of tin
to the truck graveyard
lineup of Boston Blackie nights /   deserted
right here model "T" & tomahawk
                    sometimes late in silent din of night
                    I hear
                    bagpipes /   death march
                        music of ago /   kennedy

gretsch   gretsch tune optical color-jumping gretsch
    Elvin's F-86 Sabre jet / remember Korea / Horace Silver
    the fine smooth jackets the colored boys brought back
    from the far east with "U.S. Air Force" a map of Japan
            blazing the back   —a forgotten flame

Elvin tom-tomming
bassing the chest   "E" / gretsch   "J"/gretsch
                    clashing metal mad
                    tin frantic road of roaring / gretsch
                    roar

peck morrison
the *bass* player
told me once about a drum set
with a central anchor /   every drum connected
        unable to jump or sway
        drums like the cockpit of a TXF spy plane
        ejaculator seat and all

pilot conflict
and the man elvin behind the baptismal tubs
that leap like cannons   to the slashing sound of knives
black elvin knows so well
the knives the *Daily News* displays along with the photo
of a grinning award–winning cop
the kind of knives elvin talks about
downtown by the water
and uptown
near the park.

Lee Morgan

fly by night
              black galaxy
                        friendly galaxy
fly by night

              black space/light beams
              fly by night

dance with sphere monk
in the club baron manhattan island
fly deep into night towards the light
good smoke
sings the horn
metal glass under capricorn sky

fly by night

lee morgan trilling on the ceiling
sphere monk dancing round the horseshoe bar

ghetto jazzbeaus
slick trumpeteers
jericho jammin
ass-kicking
good timing
hard bopping
good lovin
slick be bop blues and ghetto dues
so tough and tight
and beau

the white bars
cross our blue bodies
behind us glow the red lights
the black night

DUBOSE HEYWARD

Jasbo Brown

Loose heady laughter shook the humid night,
Bells jangled shrilly, and a whistle flung
A note as lonely as a soul in flight
To fail and die along a mile of river.
Then silence, while a presence moved among
The floating stars and made them swirl and quiver.

Clang-clang! A sudden world swam into view,
Dim windows banked in tiers against the dark,
And paddles threshing phosphorescent blue
Out of abysmal night; tall funnels wreathing
The scene in deeper gloom from their dark
    breathing.

Twin eyes of red and green sought out the shore,
Found it, and centered on the sagging pier.
A sleepy negro woke and raised a cheer.
A painter slapped the planks, and someone swore.

Out of the gloom the shore-line seemed to stir
And swim to greet the phantom visitor.
"Ahoy! Stand by!" Lithe, fluid shadows massed
Upon the wharf. The gang-plank rattled down.
Faint lights came running from the river town.
A door banged open on the boat and cast
An orange glare across the crowded deck,
Gashing the screen of night, secretive, vast,

And showing life, gregarious and teeming,
Bronze torsos under tatters, ridged and gleaming,
Bandanaed heads, a banjo's round blank face.
A woman's voice shrilled "Honey, I's come home."
And from the wharf: "T'ank Gawd! I's glad yo'
    come."

77

I got a song, yo' got a song,
All Gawd' chillen got a song.
Up the plank they trooped a hundred strong,
Throats belling in the warm, moist river air.
Hot laughter on the wharf, the flow and fusion
Of reds and greens and purples, then a flare
Of ecstasy that unified confusion.
"Eberybody talk about Heaben aint goin' dere,
Heaben, Heaben, goin' sing all ober Gawd'
Heaben."

From the high pilot house a voice drawled down:
"Got all your niggers off?"

                              And from below:
"Ay, ay, sir, let her go."
The gang-plank rattled up against its spars.
The tide with ponderous deliberation
Swung out the boat and drew it down the night
To lose it like a fading constellation
Destined for the graveyard of the stars.

Jasbo reeled slightly as he turned to face
The clustered lights that marked the river town.
"Gawd, I's tired," he said, and then far down
Among the shacks: "Heaben, Heaben,"

He raised his head; so, he was not alone.
The chorus throbbed in his deep baritone:
"Goin' sing all ober Gawd' Heaben,"
But no one answered. Yes, that was their way.
He ought to know by now they'd make him play
Out on the river clean from New Orleans,
But in the town they'd drop him mighty quick.
Churches were no place for muddy jeans.
He was not good enough for city ways,
And songs about their Jesus and his grace.

No, he was not. He knew it. When they whined
Their mournful hymns a trigger in his mind
Would click, and he would yearn to shout
Queer broken measures that his soul flung out
Of some recess where joy and agony
Whirled in a rhythm that he could feel and see.

The river clucked and sobbed among its piles.
A screech-owl launched a wavering ghost of sound
That ranged and circled on the watery miles
And lived to shudder in the heavy air,
Causing the lonely man upon the pier
To turn and look behind him, while his eyes
Widened and whitened. "Gawd it's lonely here."

He drew a sleeve across his sweating brow.
"All Gawd's chillen got a song," I wonder now—
That girl in New Orleans who sent him packing
Because he had to stroke the ivories
To ease the smart
That always kept devouring his heart,
Instead of heaving cotton on the boat
And earning money for her like the rest.
The sudden thought of her caught at his throat.
Old fires seared him, set his temples throbbing.
"Oh Gawd, I got de blues," he said, half sobbing.

Then, suddenly, he heard it down the shore.
A square of light leaped out, and through the door
A tinny clamor smote the heavy night.
Someone sang drunkenly, and then a fight
Flamed up and died. The door went BANG.
Something inside of Jasbo broke and sang.

They saw him reel against a shrunken moon
That hung behind him in the open door.
Scarcely at all he seemed a human being,
Lips hanging loosely and his eyes not seeing.
"My Gawd!" a woman cried, "It's Jasbo Brown,
Git off dat stool yo' empty-headed fool
An' let him play what kin."

               Somebody poured a gin,

Another, and another.
He gulped the liquid fire scarcely knowing,
Lunged heavily and slumped above the keys.
Out of the night a little wind came blowing,
A little wind, and searing memories.

"Oh Gawd, I's lonely," he moaned once, "but what's de use!"
Then crashed an aching chord and sang "I got de blues."

Oh the hypocritical
Children of the Lord,
How he jeered and mocked them
In a snarling chord.

Women who had known him,
Who had passed him by,
Once again he loved them,
Spurned them, let them die.

Bosses who had cursed him
Over Christendom
Whimpered as he flung them
Into Kingdom Come.

Out of clinkered torment
Like a rising steam,
Something spun and glittered,
Waked him, let him dream.

Showed the world, a madness
Cured by ridicule,
Praised him for a prophet,
Damned him for a fool.

Fingers conjured music
From the ivories
Into swaying bodies,
Into flexing knees.

Black face, brown face,
In the smoky light,
Gin and river women,
And the reeling night

Whirled along a rhythm
Crashing through his blood,
Jasbo, ginned and dreaming,
Stained with river mud.

Dawn, and the music tinkled out and died.
"Jus' one more Jas, here take another gin."

Two dancers dropped and sprawled,
A third stood watching with an empty grin.
The door blew open and the day smiled in.
White-footed down the river it came striding.
Beauty upon it, ancient and abiding,
Breathing of April and of jessamine.
The player rose and staggered to the street.
Oh for a place to go, a hole for hiding.

She came and stood beside him in the dew.
They watched the copper sun swing up together.
"Honey," she said at last, "I'd die for you
Most anytime yo' say when yo' are playin'."
"Yo' likes my songs?" he asked, "Dat what yo're sayin'?"
The wonder in her eyes left little doubt.
"Come home with me an' rest. Yo're clean wore out."

Down the littered street the player stumbled
With the girl beside him. Once she glanced
Up into his face and found it tranced.
His eyes had lost her, and his loose lips mumbled.
Presently, half aloud, she heard him sing
A low-keyed, minor thing:

> "Yo' got to know
> I aint de kin' for stayin'
> Always I is movin',
> Always playin'.
>
> "Life is jus' hello
> An' so-long
> For Gawd's lonely Chillen
> What got a song.
>
> "Take me home an' res' me
> In de white folks' town.
> But I got to leabe yo'
> When de boat comes down.
>
> "De boat, an' de niggers
> What love my song.
> Life is jus' hello
> An' so-long."

EDWARD HIRSCH

Art Pepper

It's the broken phrases, the fury inside him.
Squiggling alto saxophone playing out rickets
And jaundice, a mother who tried to kill him
In her womb with a coat hanger, a faltering
God-like father. The past is a bruised cloud
Floating over the houses like a prophecy,
The terrible foghorns off the shore at San Pedro.

Lightning without thunder. Years without playing.
Years of blowing out smoke and inhaling fire,
Junk and cold turkey, smacking up, the habit
Of cooking powder in spoons, the eyedroppers,
The spikes. Tracks on both arms. Tattoos.
The hospital cells at Forth Worth, the wire cages
In the L.A. County, the hole at San Quentin.

And always the blunt instrument of sex, the pain
Bubbling up inside him like a wound, the small
Deaths. The wind piercing the sheer skin
Of a dark lake at dawn. The streets at 5 a.m.
After a cool rain. The smoky blue clubs.
The chords of Parker, of Young, of Coltrane.
Playing solo means going on alone, improvising,

Hitting the notes, ringing the changes.
It's clipped phrasing and dry ice in summer,
Straining against the rhythm, speeding it up,
Loping forward and looping back, finding the curl
In the wave, the mood in the air. It's
Splintered tones and furious double timing.
It's leaving the other instruments on stage

And blowing freedom into the night, into the faces
Of emptiness that peer along the bar, ghosts,
Shallow hulls of nothingness. Hatred of God.
Hatred of white skin that never turns black.
Hatred of Patti, of Dianne, of Christine.
A daughter who grew up without him, a stranger.
Years of being strung out, years without speaking.

Pauses and intervals, silence. A fog rolling
Across the ocean, foghorns in the distance.
A lighthouse rising from the underworld.
A moon swelling in the clouds, an informer,
A twisted white mouth of light. Scars carved
And crisscrossed on his chest. The memory
Of nodding out, the dazed drop-off into sleep.

And then the curious joy of surviving, joy
Of waking up in a dusky room to a gush
Of fresh notes, a tremoring sheet of sound.
Jamming again. Careening through the scales
For the creatures who haunt the night.
Bopping through the streets in a half-light
With Laurie on his arm, a witness, a believer.

The night is going to burst inside him.
The wind is going to break loose forever
From his lungs. It's the fury of improvising,
Of going on alone. It's the fierce clarity
Of each note coming to an end, distinct,
Glistening. The alto's full-bodied laughter.
The white grief-stricken wail.

ANSELM HOLLO

Le Jazz Hot

talked to my father again in a dream he seemed happy
perhaps a little older than the last time   told me
he had discovered something called 'le jazz hot'
& found it of some interest

RICHARD HUGO

My Buddy

This then buddy is the blue routine.
You chased a fox one noon.
She hid in a golden rain.
You ran through the gold until
a rainy chill.
If that's it buddy it's a bleak routine.
What happened to you there
may never happen again.

So say buddy it is a bleak routine.
The word caves in your skull.
All eyes give you chill.
The fox shows up on the moon
on the horizon, laughing you blind
painting the routine orange.
What happens to you now
happens again.

Say you deserve it. That's a good routine.
I'm nothing, see,
to the storming worms.
The fox died warm in ground.
Now she's gone tell what a bitch she was
loud in a red routine
and say it never happened to you.
Don't show no pain.

Sweet dear buddy it's a gray routine.
A girl rode in off the prairie
a very snuggly cuddly
had a neat twitch coming in
ran off with another man.
Sorry buddy for the brute routine.
For you it can never happen
over and over again.

One rain more and glory afternoon
complete with gin
and trees gone nuts in the gale
that's always whipping even in heat

when you sweat like the dog you are
when you sweat and swear at me buddy
in my underwear
hoping I have your hair.

Boogie boogie buddy. Scarey boo.
Here's a foxy ghost for you.
One with a heart big as a smirk
and a hot toe in your ear.
You're still my buddy
aren't you?
Sorry. A bizarre machine.
Stay away from my gears.

Hell old buddy back to the routine.
I mean routine routine.
The time clock tied to your dong.
The same bitch punching your card
that very snuggly cuddly
off with another man.
Someday buddy you'll say the wrong thing.
We'll never be friends again.

What to do blue buddy now you're gone?
Sing a song? Sing of a lost routine?
Buddy on skins and me in my cups
crying play it, play it again.
No sense losing a tear to the floor
with a mug of beer in your hand
and the blind proprietor yelling
go on, buddy, go on.

LYNDA HULL

Lost Fugue for Chet

Chet Baker, Amsterdam, 1988

A single spot slides the trumpet's flare then stops
    at that face, the extraordinary ruins thumb-marked
with the hollows of heroin, the rest chiaroscuroed.
    Amsterdam, the final gig, canals & countless

stone bridges arc, glimmered in lamps. Later this week
     his Badlands face, handsome in a print from thirty
years ago, will follow me from the obituary page
     insistent as windblown papers by the black cathedral

of St. Nicholas standing closed today: pigeon shit
     & feathers, posters swathing tarnished doors, a litter
of syringes. Junkies cloud the gutted railway station blocks
     & dealers from doorways call *coca, heroina,* some throaty

foaming harmony. A measured inhalation, again
     the sweet embouchure, metallic, wet stem. Ghostly,
the horn's improvisations purl & murmur
     the narrow *strasses* of *Rosse Buurt,* the district rife

with purse-snatchers, women alluring, desolate, poised
     in blue windows, Michelangelo boys, hair spilling
fluent running chords, mares' tails in the sky green
     & violet. So easy to get lost, these cavernous

brown cafés. Amsterdam, & its spectral fogs, its
     bars & softly shifting tugboats. He builds once more
the dense harmonic structure, the gabled houses.
     Let's get lost. Why court the brink & then step back?

After surviving, what arrives? So what's the point
     when there are so many women, creamy callas with single
furled petals turning in & in upon themselves
     like variations, nights when the horn's coming

genius riffs, metal & spit, that rich consuming rush
     of good dope, a brief languor burnishing
the groin, better than any sex. Fuck Death.
     In the audience, there's always this gaunt man, cigarette

in hand, black Maserati at the curb, waiting,
     the fast ride through mountain passes, descending with
no rails between asphalt & precipice. Inside, magnetic
     whispering *take me there, take me.* April, the lindens

& horse chestnuts flowering, cold white blossoms
     on the canal. He's lost as he hears those inner voicings,
a slurred veneer of chords, molten, fingering
     articulate. His glance below Dutch headlines, the fall

"accidental" from a hotel sill. Too loaded. What do you do
     at the brink? Stepping back in time, I can only
imagine the last hit, lilies insinuating themselves
     up your arms, leaves around your face, one hand vanishing

sabled to shadow. The newsprint photo & I'm trying
    to recall names, songs, the sinuous figures, but facts
don't matter, what counts is out of pained dissonance,
    the sick vivid green of backstage bathrooms, out of

broken rhythms – and I've never forgotten, never –
    this is the tied-off vein, this is 3 A.M. terror
thrumming, this is the carnation of blood clouding
    the syringe, you shaped *summer rains across the quays*

of Paris, flame suffusing jade against a girl's
    dark ear. From the trumpet, pawned, redeemed, pawned again
you formed one wrenching blue arrangement, a phrase endlessly
    complicated as that twilit dive through smoke, applause,

the pale haunted rooms. Cold chestnuts flowering April
    & you're falling from heaven in a shower of eighth notes
to the cobbled street below & foaming dappled horses
    plunge beneath the still green waters of the Grand Canal.

Ornithology

    Gone to seed, ailanthus, the poverty
        tree. Take a phrase, then
    fracture it, the pods' gaudy nectarine shades
            ripening to parrots taking flight, all crest
    and tail feathers.
                    A musical idea.
                            Macaws
        scarlet and violet,
                            tangerine as a song
    the hue of sunset where my street becomes water

    and down shore this phantom city skyline's
        mere hazy silhouette. The alto's
    liquid geometry weaves *a way of thinking,*
            a way of breaking
    synchronistic
                    through time
                                so the girl
        on the corner
                        has the bones of my face,
    the old photos, beneath the Kansas City hat,

black fedora lifting hair off my neck
   cooling the sweat of a night-long tidal
pull from bar to bar the night we went
     to find Bird's grave. Eric's chartreuse
perfume. That
               poured-on dress
                        I lived days
    and nights inside,
               made love
and slept in, a mesh and snurr of zipper
down the back. Women smoked the boulevards
   with gardenias after-hours, asphalt shower-
slick, ozone charging air with sixteenth
    notes, that endless convertible ride to find
the grave
        whose sleep and melody
                      wept neglect
    enough to torch us
             for a while
through snare-sweep of broom on pavement,

the rumpled musk of lover's sheets, charred
   cornices topping crosstown gutted buildings.
Torches us still—cat screech, matte blue steel
    of pistol stroked across the victim's cheek
where fleet shoes
           jazz this dark
               and peeling
   block, that one.
          Vine Street, Olive.
We had the music, but not the pyrotechnics—

rhinestone straps lashing my shoes, heels sinking
   through earth and Eric in casual drag,
mocha cheekbones rouged, that flawless
    plummy mouth. A style for moving,
heel tap and
        lighter flick,
            lion moan
  of buses pulling away
             through the static
brilliant fizz of taffeta on nyloned thighs.

Light mist, etherous, rinsed our faces
   and what happens when
you touch a finger to the cold stone
     that jazz and death played
down to?
          Phrases.
                Take it all
   and break forever—
              a man
with gleaming sax, an open sill in summertime,
and the fire escape's iron zigzag tumbles
   crazy notes to a girl cooling her knees,
wearing one of those dresses no one wears
     anymore, darts and spaghetti straps, glitzy
fabrics foaming
           an iron bedstead.
                  The horn's
   alarm, then fluid brass chromatics.
                Extravagant
ailanthus, the courtyard's poverty tree is spike

and wing, slate-blue
           mourning dove,
                sudden cardinal flame.

If you don't live it, it won't come out your horn.

T. R. HUMMER

Poem in the Shape of a Saxophone

Refracted through years, this neon light comes back,
Blue in the etched lines of a bar's lead-glass windows.
Somebody in an apartment, high
Over the asthmatic August streets of one more city
In the whipped-out heart
          of the old northeast,
Tries to make the horn sound sweet, like Hawk.
That's hip to know, who he wants to sound like,
What it is in his jaw that trembles a little wrong

Back of the reed—but the woman on the barstool knows.
She is a woman I loved
                              for what she remembered
About the breath, how if you don't move it
Exactly right the tones won't round, how the tongue
Has to do what it has to do precisely.
Now she sits on a barstool in the past, where I put her,
Blowing a smoke ring
                              delicately stained with the predictable
Bloodred lipstick of the early 1940s.
I put her there and I keep her there,
Dressed in blue silk she would never have chosen herself,
Years before she was born. I want her to hear the stillborn
Choruses waffle over
                              the apartment window ledge and down
Into the street, into the bar where she sits, theme music
From a bad old movie. I want her there so I can speak of her
In the past tense, where it's safe, where nobody cares
If I say *I loved,* or if the horn in the high window lifts
Its minor third a shade
                              indecorously sharp.
Her hair in this light takes the tone of brass, sweeps
Its unnatural metallic curve past her shoulder, cheap,
You'll say, and easy, but you don't understand
The timbre of love, gold in this nonexistent air,
The uterine mouth
                              of the horn's bell where the tune crowns
And comes out crippled, a clubfoot kid with a kickball,
An old man blowing a blues-harp at the mouth of the subway.
This is how I imagine the place where I keep her,
The organized violence I commit on ordinary space.
This is what men and women
                              do to each other: make
Breathy worlds and expect each other to live there,
Beautifully improvised. This is why
When the light comes down blue from the neon sign
Sketched in the dry shape of a cool martini
To touch the gin in her glass,
                              it wavers off-key
And she frowns, she stubs out her cigarette,
She pays her tab and goes home, knowing where she's going,
Slow-dancing into some present where her husband and children

Listen to whatever music the stereo spins,
Where the houses love wants
                              stagger along the made-up
Streets of the suburbs, lawn by sunlit lawn—
And just as she's out of range, the man
With the horn overhead takes another breath, touches
The reed with his tongue, lays his hands
On the keys.
                Now, at street level, light comes down
In final abstract perfection on the right side of lovers
Walking perpendicular to what I will first call
Sunset, then blackout, Saturday night
Where the man upstairs touches the unreal gold
Curve of the horn's cold body,
                              starts counting time.

ANGELA JACKSON

Billie in Silk

I have nothing to say to you, Billie Holiday.
You do not look at me when I try to speak to you.
You cannot look me in the eye. Your eyes
look elsewhere.
Your steamy mouth sewn up with red tears
is poised to speak
to someone.
The orchid in your hair grows, grows like
a spider turning herself inside out.
The shadow hangs
into your eye.

I have smiled the way you
do not smile.
I was just out of love,
and cold.
I was naked, beyond caring.
My smile, like yours, was a wry line
beside my steamy mouth.
My eyes, like yours, didn't look at me,

I only saw the fall
from
grace.

> (You lay down with music in the leaves.
> You wrapped him in leaves, in sheets.
> Your legs lindyed around him. Young
> then old. Do not be deceived. The
> thunder of the spider is no small
> thing. You had your way with music,
> and ate him. The memory hot
> in your belly. Ours.)

> *You never want to let her leave.*
> *She. The voice deceives.*
> *You could hurt it.*
> *It would kill you*
> *too.*
> *The dragline seeking*
> *curving above Surprise.*
> *Below*
> *Just so.*
> *Size is not the issue.*
> *Volume not*
> *the question. A hairline*
> *fracture in the Silence*
> *in which nothing rests.*
> *The voice deceives.*
> *Every thing*
> *swings.*

I have something to say to you, Billie Holiday.
Sew up your breathing, then send it back to me.
Fluent and ruminating the source of such anguish.

Look into my eyes.

If only it were not so lonely to be black and bruised
by an early-morning dream
that lifts the mouth to sing.

Here is an orchid, spideresque-petaled, glorious,
full of grace.

My mouth is on fire. Let it burn.

Make/n My Music

my colored child/hood wuz mostly music
  celebrate/n be/n young an Black (but we din know it)
   scream/n up the wide alleys
 an holler/n afta the walla-mellon-man.

  sun-rest time
  my mama she wuz yell/n
   (all ova the block
     sang/n fa us
  ta git our butts in
       side.

we grew up run/n jazz rhythms
   an watch/n mr. wiggins downstairs
    knock the blues up side   his woman's
       head
we rocked.   an the big boys they snuck
an rolled   dice /   in the hallways at nite.

i mean. we laughed love.   an the teen
   agers they jus slow dragged thru smokey
       tunes.
   life wuz a ordinary miracle   an
   have/n fun wuzn no temptation

   we just dun it.
an   u know
i think we grew.   thru them spirit-uals
   the saint-tified folks wud git happy off
   of even if we *wuz* just clown/n
   when we danced the grizzly bear an
   felt good when the reverend
   wid the black cadillac   said:

   let the holy ghost come in
   side you

that music make you/feel sooo/ good!

any how   i wuz a little colored girl
   then . . .

so far
my Black woman/hood ain't been noth/n but music

       i found billie
            holiday   an learned
                  how
                  to cry.

Ohnedaruth

my throats
a hungry saxophone. longing
the cold train.   of yo breath
             release me.
i am. one diamond-silvered note.

yo mouth knows secret songs.
i remember.

RICHARD JACKSON

Shadows

Why is there something rather than nothing?
  —Parmenides

What a consoling poem this will be if the roadside
crows that scatter into pines as each car passes,
that rise like the souls of the dead in Van Gogh's wide
and confused heaven, are not the signs of your loss.
What a consoling poem this might be if I could remember
the first secret place where the pitiful world did not,
as Flaubert says it does, surface in terrible error
like the bloated bodies of dogs in a stream near his retreat
at Rouen, those poor shadows of the dead, despite
the stones tied to their necks, and surface in the sentences
Flaubert wrote trying to find a secret place for each right
word, a place that did not mean the old disgust for happiness.
I thought I had seen death. I see instead those rising crows

again, remember your leaving, and, scattered here, in shadows
that fall across this page, figures I'd forgotten, shadows
that seem to rise from the faded newsprint, that seem to show
how each private loss is part of a larger loss we might
remember,—yesterday's news is the young boy in Providence
R.I., who followed the consoling words of some killer one night
into woods where animals later tore off his face, or two Palestinians,
two boys, faces covered, who followed one street or another
with a crowd of protesters and were shot, or how, unable to let
death take him, a Bantu tribesman clutched the dirt of his father,
lifting himself again so the Pretoria soldiers could not forget.
Listen, it is nearly dawn here. I wish all these losses
could hide in the shifting forms of these words, that you could hide
in their dream that tries to tell you not to abandon your past
in a few clothes on the shore, no place left to hide.

I didn't know, when you left, about poor Flaubert never finding
the words to dominate the absurd sounds of parrots he kept
hearing, the plaintive sounds of cicadas that always haunted
him, how he would mutilate phrases, how he'd shift sentences,
how each word was, he wrote, an "endless farewell to life,"
crossing out repetitions that meant he had only one voice,
that meant, really, hearing the endless terror of his own voice.
I didn't know, then, about Van Gogh, who was finding
in an asylum, while Flaubert tried to write an asylum for his life,
a style to hold off death, a style that he feared, that he kept
even from his brother. I hadn't read, then, those poor sentences
to Theo, haunted by the power of color and shape, haunted
by shadows of enemies he invented, the way the birds haunt
his last painting, *Crows Over a Wheatfield,* where the lost voice
of Christ seems to dissolve into darkness that moment his sentence
was finished, those crows that could be flying towards us, finding
only our losses, or up towards heaven, or maybe they keep
wavering, flying both ways at once, the way Van Gogh's life
would, as he himself knew, painting, he wrote, his own life
in theirs. I can't help but wonder how those crows haunt
all his last paintings. I believe he must have found a way to keep
a secret place somewhere on each canvas, the way Christ's voice
seems to hide beneath the thick paint. I believe he must have found
how the birds carry the painting away from itself, as Flaubert's sentences
were meant to lead him away from what he called the sentence
of his life. And because he saw a halo shimmering around each life

or object the way he had as a young preacher, what did Van Gogh find,
what consolation against all that pain? I am still haunted
by that faceless boy in Providence, the African without a voice,
the Palestinian boys kept from their homes, these deaths that keep
announcing their obscene selves. Like Flaubert, I'm going to keep
trying to find some style, some shape for these sentences.
I believe I can hear, in Van Gogh's painting, the poor voice
of Christ which is the voice, too, of Flaubert, and these lost lives
that haunt me now. I believe that the last demon that haunted
Van Gogh was his fear that, outside his frames, nothing was found
to keep the "troubled skies" from his life, nothing even
in his sentences to Theo—"what's the use?" he asked hauntingly,
finally, like the voice of Christ, crying to be found.

Listen, I am writing to you now, on this table crossed
by shadows, that the answer is anyone hearing your voice,
anyone hoping the next news of you is not your loss,
trying by these repetitions to call you back, though the place
keeps shifting because I can't hide the world Flaubert, at Rouen,
fought inside each phrase, and you wouldn't believe a story
with no form for suicide or death. Here I am again
thinking of Van Gogh, listening to Lightnin' Hopkins say
the blues are everywhere, the blues are us, these stories
he sings on the scratched tape, the stories we read
about Van Gogh, the headlines, the poems, the way
the blues rhythms never change, 4/4, as if we needed
something that constant against our fears, as if we knew
how much these sad stories showed us what it means
to go on. Here I am again, listening to the blues,
starting to understand it is my own despair I mean
to fight. Last night, I stood on the bridge where a friend
dove into the shadows of the Tennessee and was afraid
I understood. I was thinking of the faceless boy again,
remembering how the man who found him by the pond where he lay
face down, turned him over, saw what the animals had done
and knelt in prayer, knelt for the pity of it, for the faces
of everyone dead or missing, knowing how he must go on.
I was thinking, too, how the mothers of the Palestinian boys
must also have knelt, must have touched the life
leaking from them, must also have prayed, unwrapped
the cloth around their heads hoping some other life,
not a son's, was missing. I have been thinking how the map

of this table, ever since you left, scatters the shadows
of fears this poem tries to shape, and how Van Gogh's
pictures, the dark secret places in Flaubert's phrases, show
all our words as a care for life, a color we have to hold.

I can't forget that faceless boy. I can't stop wondering
what last thing he touched or saw. I get up, punch
another tape into the player, Charlie Parker, "the Bird,"
taking off into rhythms and harmonies more unpredictable
than Van Gogh's crows—taking notes from what he touched or saw—
dogs barking, the hiss of a radiator, the sudden squeal
of a train's brakes, the rhythm and harmonies of the unpredictable
drunk shifting in a doorway, changing every sad thing
so that the dog's barking, the hiss of the radiator, the squeal
of brakes becomes not a sign of loneliness or loss, but joy,
the notes shifting like Flaubert's words, like the drunk in the doorway,
discovering in each phrase and note some secret place
among the flattened fifths meaning either loss or joy,
among the odd intervals of chords his alto sax remembers,
until he fell asleep for good in an armchair in New York,
nearly 35, "I'm just a husk," he said, in the end, just a phrase
or interval you remember, and I do, in this poem for you,
taking these hints from the flights of the bird, Charlie Parker,
who lived beyond death in each note, each husk, each phrase,
above the deaths of the boy, the Palestinians, the tribesmen.

I remember last summer, finding an old sax player
just waking among the remnants of fieldstone cellars
some quarry workers left half a century ago outside
Gloucester, Mass., a place called *Dogtown,* where he tried
among the sounds of stray dogs Parker would have loved
to remember the clear notes of the alto sax rising above
the trees, above his memory of the war, unable to sleep
without checking the perimeter, each hour, to keep
all the shadows named and held, unable to sleep at all
if it rained because he couldn't hear the enemy's footfall.
It could have been you there, he said, and I know,
I know all our shadows, *it could have been you.*
And I am remembering the Bantu tribesman, how he could
tell immediately that the difference between dirt and blood
no longer mattered, that the lost children he fought for,
the child detained for questioning and found weeks later

among the smoldering garbage, his tongue cut out
for talking to newsmen, were what his death might be about,
a death that gathered above the tin roofs as the past gathered
—maybe the way it gathered in the eyes of the sax player
who could not forget, as he told it, the way his base
camp was overrun, the way, after a while, the haze
he was seeing was not dawn, not even the smoke of rifles,
but the unbelievable smoke of bodies burning, and the terrible
vapor that rose from open wounds, the sickening stink
that took the place of words, screams, whatever he tried to think.
When things were bad, he said, he could remember the service
for William Williams in New Orleans, how the entire brass
had gathered for the long march to Carrolton cemetery—
the Eureka Brass Band—with it slow dirges, its heavy
hymn notes to "In the Sweet Bye and Bye," the trombones
leading the way, he and his father among the baritone
horns of the second rank—and how they danced on the way
home to "St. Louis Blues," music, he said, you could raise
the dead with, as now, he just wanted once more to hear
the consoling notes of Parker, some sound to drive away his fear.

Listen, I have tried to find for us a shape for all this grief,
a form to make, as Parker and Van Gogh did, our fear
into a strength. It may be that any form is a kind of belief
that the losses, the shadows on this table, the enemy we fear
when the world goes dark, can be contained beyond our moment.
In Berea, Ohio, once, I came across an old graveyard
next to a quarry, centered by a concubine pine, a tree
that grew around its own cones and branches that were bent
around the trunk, as if the tree took as its form the discarded
parts of its own past and future. Now I want to believe
the long embrace of that tree, to touch my hands to your face,
I am touching my own face now, unable to forget that faceless
boy, the frightened sax player, hoping to find here some place
where we can kneel before these shadows, where we can bless
and embrace our pasts. I am blessing the past of a friend, torn coat,
hovering on a doorstep in Belgrade before he escaped the Russians,
who would twist gunpowder out of shells to sell to gangs for bread,
who watched a kneeling soldier smile to slit a prisoner's throat,
who chose not the Danube, but life. Not long ago I knelt in
the park where he played, one secret place where finally the dead
were only distant shadows. I was feeding the few ragged crows

that could have been Van Gogh's birds, leaving them a little bread
and cheese, thinking again of you, of your sadness, of how
form may be only, as Whitman said, another name for the body,
for all the secret places we contain, the only consolation we
    have known—
and I was gathering you around me, building my own secret place
inside you, feeling you move again unpredictably, like Parker's
rhythms, the shifts in Flaubert's sentences, knowing, having known,
that this poem begins in your body and ends in the same place,
feeling the world move, trying to stay this way forever.

DAVID JAUSS

After the End of the World

Sun Ra and His Intergalactic Research Arkestra, Berlin, 1976

The Arkestra glitters in their Saturn gowns
and galaxy caps, cosmic rosaries round their necks.
Dancers, acrobats, a fire-eater.
Beside Sun Ra's organ, a telescope on its tripod,
aimed toward the stars beyond the ceiling
he wills to lift off, like a spaceship. Squinting
one eye, opening wide the other. *Welcome
to the eighth ring of Saturn,*

home sweet home. Snickers. If only
they could hear his *Music from the Private Library
of the Creator of the Universe,* they'd know
how homesick he was. He'd recorded it twice
but the tape stayed blank. It was His property,
he could dig that. Forbidden fruit.
Solaristic Precept Number Two: The sequence of life
is sound diminished to its smallest point:

silence.
The smell of butter rum Lifesavers: Coltrane
here again. 1959, the Sutherland Lounge in Chicago,
reading his precepts, laughing but not laughing too
and later playing, now and then,

99

scattered phrases from the *Private Library.* A citizen
of the universe. *Welcome, John.*
Take a seat in the Eternal Thought

and listen to the Future with us.
Solaristic Precept Number One: Thorough consideration
of the patterns of the past because coming events
cast their shadows before. That's why
you have to give up your life
before you die. Anybody can give it up and die
but to keep on living after, that's the test,
ain't it, John? Pythagoras,

Tycho Brahe, Galileo,
all of them medicine men from outer space
who died into new lives. Behind him the Arkestra finishes
"It's After the End of the World," and he rises,
a black sun, to bow and bless the Berliners who do not know
the impossible is possible because the impossible
is a thought and every thought
is real. *I've come from Saturn*

to make you citizens of Infinity.
How else could he, a boy of seven in Birmingham,
the first time he saw music, play it?
John, you could tell them, if only you could speak
once more on your saxophone, if only
the future weren't so loud
it deafens everyone
doomed to life on this planet.

Black Orchid

Miles Davis, New York, August, 1950

for Lynda Hull

Tonight he's playing the Black Orchid,
the old Onyx where before his habit
he played with Bird, looking cleaner
than a motherfucker, Brooks Brothers suit,
marcelled hair, trumpet floating over

that hurricane of sixteenth notes no one
could have played sober—19, a dentist's son,
on stage with *Bird* and laying down shit
nobody ever heard before or since!—but now
his fourth cap of heroin's wearing off,
its petals closing up inside his chest so tight
he can barely breathe. Drunk again,
Bud hangs heavy over the keys, left hand
jabbing chords that break his right hand's
waterfall arpeggios: "April in Paris,"
and that strangely tropical odor of coconut
and lime in rum comes back to Miles,
the smell of Paris, Juliette Greco's sweet lips
as she sang, each syllable a kiss
for him alone. *Juliette,*
his trumpet moans, *her small hands*
on the small of my back, long hair black
on the white pillow . . . Even Sartre
tried to talk him into marrying her
but he'd gone back to America, to Irene,
and a habit. And though numerology proved
he was a perfect six, the Devil's number,
he drove the Blue Demon, top down, to East St. Louis,
Irene silent beside him, the kids crying
in the back seat, one thousand miles
to escape heroin and the memory
of Juliette's white shoulder. But now
he's back, alone, long sleeves
hiding fresh tracks on his forearms,
and it's not Bird but Sonny who's unraveling
the melody, looking in it for a way
to put it all back together again.
Then Wardell leaps in, *This is it, man,*
can't you hear *it?* They're dueling
like Ground Hog and Baby, the junky tapdancers
who buck-and-winged for dope on the sidewalk
outside Minton's, feet turning desperation
into music, and Miles joins them, his mute
disguising the notes he fluffs. He sounds
as bad as Fats, last May when they recorded
Birdland All-Stars. Glassy-eyed, nose running,
Fat Girl had to strain to hit notes

101

he used to own. 26 and just two
months to live. *I'm going to kick this shit,*
Miles vowed the night Fats died,
but here he is, blowing a borrowed horn
because he pawned his own to play
a syringe's one-valve song. If only
he'd stayed, if only he'd never come back . . .
Behind him, Art plays Paris dark
as a jungle, and Miles falls into her pale arms,
the dark hotel room, and he's lost, lost
and free, released from some burden he's borne
across the ocean, to this bed, this woman,
a burden that, lifting, lifts him
like music, one clear unwavering note piercing
the silence that defines it . . .
When he tries to explain, she tells him
he's an *existentialiste,* like Jean-Paul. "To hell
with philosophy," he says, "Let's fuck."
And she laughs, her mouth a red flower
opening under his. Then he kisses
two whole notes out of his horn, their beauty
painful as they vanish into the swirling
smoke of the Orchid, each note
unfurling, an orchid itself, its petals
falling and settling on the nodding heads
of grinning white Americans
who will never understand jazz, or Paris,
or him. He closes his eyes,
and for as long as his solo lasts,
it's not August, it's not New York,
and he is not dying.

LANCE JEFFERS

How High the Moon

(first the melody, clean and hard,
and the flat slurs are faint;
the downknotted mouth, tugged in deprecation,
is not there. But near the end of the first chorus
the slurs have come

with the street of the quiet pogrom:
the beat of the street talk flares strong,
the scornful laughter and the gestures cut the air.)

"Blow! Blow!" the side-men cry,

and the thin black young man with an old man's face
lungs up
the tissue of a trumpet from his deep-cancered corners,
racks out a high and searing curse!
    Full from the sullen grace of his street it sprouts:
        NEVER YOUR CAPTIVE!

Nina Simone

this brown woman's voice,
this blackwheat voice
this blackthigh voice
this blackbreast voice:
far far in the dim of me I hear her in the dark field
    of the slavery South:
gowned in burlap, barefoot,
head down, a musing smile on her lips:
out into the fields before the dawn she goes alone:
she gazes into the trees swaying in the slowly-draining night:
sudden grief pierces her torso and she laughs scornfully:

Now she stands before a microphone and
    feels the echoes of her slavery past:
an ache across her torso and a desolating laugh:
she throws back her head to sing and her teeth whiten
    the bloodsea of her mouth.

JUNE JORDAN

October 23, 1983

for a.b.t.

The way she played the piano
        the one listening was the one taken
        the one taken was the one
            into the water/

103

watching the foam
find the beautiful boulders
dark
easily liquid
and true as the stone
of that meeting/molecular
elements of lust
distilled by the developing
sound
sorrow
sound
fused by the need of the fingers
to note down
to touch upon
to span
to isolate
to pound
to syncopate
to sound
sorrow
sound
among the waters
gathering
corpuscular/exquisite
constellations tuning among waves
the soul itself
pitched atonal but below
the constellations tuning among waves
the soul itself

a muscular/exquisite

matter of tactful
             exact
             uproarious
heart
collecting the easily dark
liquid
look
of the beautiful boulders

in that gathering
   that water

ALLISON JOSEPH

My Father's Heroes

He gloried in the feats
of Cool Papa Bell, quickest
man in the Negro Leagues,
able, Dad bragged,
to flick off a light switch,
then dart into bed
before the room went dark.
Praising the fast feet
of the Nicholas Brothers,
he called me to their
rapid-fire acrobatics,
but saved his true love
for Peg Leg Bates,
who'd pound out a furious rhythm
on his wooden leg,
dazzling everyone
with leaps and bounds.
I never saw my father
anywhere near a piano,
but he still schooled me
about Jimmy Rushing—
"Mister Five by Five"
who stood five feet tall
and just as wide,
had me humming Jelly Roll's
creole jazz though he'd never
been near New Orleans,
made certain I knew the difference
between Fats Domino and Fats Waller,
played me the Harlem rhapsodies
of Ellington so loud I thought
the orchestra had come to visit,
Sir Duke himself in our living
room, elegant in top hat, tails.
To Dad, Satchmo and Satchel Paige
both deserved praise; equal
adulation given to Louie Jordan

as he belted out rhythm and blues
about hard-headed women,
the hi-di-ho of Cab Calloway
as he spun tales of Minnie the Moocher,
regal in yards of zoot suit,
and to the sublime grace of Mr. B
crooning smoother than any white man.
Coleman Hawkins, Lester Young,
Bird and Diz all came to play
from our raspy console hi-fi,
its needle worn, jumping over scratches.

But some mornings,
I'd wake to hear a woman's voice
filling our rooms with trembling
love songs, a voice so female
even I understood, even though
the language was French.
This, he'd say, *is Piaf,*
the little sparrow,
and I'd listen to her
send sorrows through our house
and I knew what touched my father
wasn't always race, wasn't color.
Somehow he knew I needed
to hear this woman sing
from her fragile bones,
her sound silencing us both,
as her crowds in Paris must have
when they saw her tiny figure
on the stage, bent over to sing
the last vestiges of a ballad,
the last words
she'd give them.

ROBERT KELLY

Newark

John Coltrane died this morning, LeRoi's in jail.

Whatever you say of the daytime
it gives you a taste
for the obvious

the places where
night is
filled with a different wisdom

but on deck, both feet firm
in the sunshine
Coltrane died this morning
& had nothing to say about this

                     But at star-rise (she said)

the rifles
firing into the sky behind the movie house
shooting up the airport
24 (to pick a number
out of the air) dead in Newark,
                 Coltrane dead & all

our flights canceled
out of the air
        but Roi, where is the night, where is the dark
brooding hot snake-mother gives us birth
where no sun comes to distinguish our skins?

                           at star-rise
(she said) we shot together,
light of Unukalhai, Snake-Neck,
light of the seven weepers
               weeping bullshit
               all over the Jersey lawns

(no rain . suspension of thick sweet New York air,
where had he been, where did he get the .38s
anyhow?
        Do you propose to shoot me down? up?
at star-fall (she said) the smog so thick.

can't tell one mother from another, what
.38s?
                        she said at star-fall the light began,
people moved out of their houses, the man died,
                                            a man is his meat

no meat in the night
if we get to the night together
we'll be somewhere
                        (action from star-rise,
cool it, the troops pulled out,
a work accomplished
some black men dead, a poet in jail,

check the famous empty
dawn rising over the meadows
                        (she said "I'm sorry I was ever
for them, I say take out machine guns & shoot them down")
cool dawn . cool
                cell they work somebody over in
(she said he asked for it) (did you see any guns?)
                                            Trane

rode out on a bad rime, bad shit
they shoot us to live on
                        The words
break down,
                he made it
say itself inside our heads.

Ode to Language

To put on shoes and be sophisticated
—it really was a creamy trumpet
Miles Davis made—or gleam waxy
and smile along the El-shadowed street
through all the synaesthesias of weary language
patient, at our command, like an old dog.

Faithful animal! Endure
Tehran, Stella by Starlight, Nautilus
machines, the skanky fantasies
of men no longer young, the rough

108

edge of graffiti, borrowed vices
of exurban novelists, the price of glass.

Break me. Come to me
with burrs in your fur, tell me
where everything has ever been.
Growl at me if I sleep, wake me
with your dependable craziness.
Birds plummet and you fetch them
wet from your mouth. Women weep
in San Francisco. Only you

are ever different.

KEORAPETSE KGOSITSILE

Acknowledgement

after & for John Coltrane

I said a while back
John Coltrane. Trane
And the tracks. What
Womb they lead you to
Is your life nourished,
Or pushed against the walls
Of your festering decay

TRANE, Goodgod, we been
dead so long and missed
the Trane. Listen here:
There is music, will always
be in spite of songs that die
or dry up like crust over any sore

John Coltrane, they say
he died, the hasty fools
that pick his bones for a quick
dollar, John Coltrane, who is
a door, how could he die
if you have ears!

For Art Blakey and the Jazz Messengers

For the sound we revere
we dub you art as continuum
as spirit as sound of depth
here to stay

          In my young years
I heard you bopping and weaving
messages I could only walk to
where wood mates with skin

I would have dubbed you godhead
but your sound rolled and pealed:
I am the drumhead even though
Blue Note don't care nothing
bout nothing but profit

How you sound is
who you are
where your ear
leans moaning or bopping
from the amen corner
of chicken and dumpling
memories and places

In my young years
I would have dubbed you
something strange as god
of opiate heaven
of brutal contact
of bible and rifle memories

But the drumhead rolled my name:
How you sound is
who you are
like drumsound
backing back to root
roosting at the meeting place
the time that has always been here

Even here where wood
mates with skin on wax
to make memory, to place us
even in this hideous place

pp–ppounding pp–ppounding
the ss–sssounds of who
we are even in this place
of strange and brutal design

YUSEF KOMUNYAKAA

Speed Ball

Didn't Chet Baker know
They made each great white hope
Jump hoops of fire on the edge
Of midnight gigs that never happened?

Miles hipped him at The Lighthouse
About horse, said not to feel guilty
About *Down Beat* in '53. Chet stole
Gasoline to sniff, doctored with Beiderbecke's

Chicago style. But it wasn't long
Before he was a toothless lion
Gazing up at his face like a stranger's
Caught by tinted lens & brass. Steel-

Blue stare from Oklahoma whispering for
"A kind of high that scares everyone
To death." Maybe a bop angel, Slim
Greer, pulled him from that hotel window.

Twilight Seduction

Because Duke's voice
    was smooth as new silk
        edged with Victorian lace, smooth

as Madame Zajj nude
    beneath her mink coat,
        I can't help but run

my hands over you at dusk.
    Hip to collarbone, right ear
        lobe to the sublime. Simply

111

because Jimmy Blanton
    died at twenty-one
        & his hands on the bass

still make me ashamed
    to hold you like an upright
        & a cross worked into one

embrace. Fingers pulse
    at a gold zipper, before
        the brain dances the body

into a field of poppies.
    Duke knew how to listen
        to colors, for each sigh shaped

out of sweat & blame,
    knew a Harlem airshaft
        could recall the whole

night in an echo: prayers,
    dogs barking, curses & blessings.
        Plunger mute tempered

by need & plea. He'd search
    for a flaw, a small scar,
        some mark of perfect

difference for his canvas.
    I hold your red shoes,
        one in each hand to balance

the sky, because Duke
    loved Toulouse Lautrec's
        nightlife. Faces of women

woven into chords scribbled
    on hotel stationery—blues,
        but never that unlucky

green. April 29th
    is also my birthday,
        the suspicious wishbone

snapped between us,
    & I think I know why
        a pretty woman always

lingered *at the bass*
   clef end of the piano.
      Tricky Sam coaxed

an accented wa–wa
   from his trombone, coupled
      with Cootie & Bubber,

& Duke said, *Rufus,*
   give me some ching-chang
      & sticks on the wood.

I tell myself the drum
   can never be a woman,
      even if her name's whispered

across skin. Because
   nights at the Cotton Club
      shook on the bone,

because Paul Whiteman
   sat waiting for a riff
      he could walk away with

as feathers twirled
   among palm trees, because
      Duke created something good

& strong out of thirty pieces
   of silver like a spotlight
      on conked hair,

because so much flesh
   is left in each song,
      because women touch

themselves to know
   where music comes from,
      my fingers trace

your lips to open up
   the sky & let in
      the night.

OLIVER LAGRONE

I Heard the Byrd

It was a bash!
It was a smash!
It was a blast . . . !
I heard the Byrd.
Memory came in
To help recall again
By image and by word:
Said my old friend,
"The fame is in the name" . . .
Broken reverie of a silver bell—
The muted trumpet casts its spell—
Rubdown with a velvet glove
And,
Gabriel's blast from heaven above
All the way to edge of hell . . .

It was a flight of wings . . .
Names and birds again . . .
They called one
The Lone Eagle—
Name for a name . . .
Another, The Yard Bird.
And now a third—
The Byrd I only lately
Saw and heard—
Together,
Took me up by myself
With thousands on a sky-hi trip
Left us on a Shaky shelf
Then shook it!

Shook it!
Shook the ship to make us flip . . .
And dropped us with the sharp git-pick
Paced with bass and fretted snare
And notes—
Ivory's melodic rhymes to everywhere . . .
Blue, black-white and silver-gold
All stations where the many-souled

Drawn into family of just one care . . .
To join the beat
To keep the sound
Made by the 'Bird's' appointed rounds . . .
No time or aim for mass conclusion
Flight was the magic call,
The 'Bird-time's' music fusion . . .

Fly on, Bird,
Fly on!
The fame is in the name . . .
I heard the Bird.

VACHEL LINDSAY

The Jazz of This Hotel

Why do I curse the jazz of this hotel?
I like the slower tom-toms of the sea;
I like the slower tom-toms of the thunder;
I like the more deliberate dancing knee
Of outdoor love, of outdoor talk and wonder.
I like the slower, deeper violin
Of the wind across the fields of Indian corn;
I like the far more ancient violoncello
Of whittling loafers telling stories mellow
Down at the village grocery in the sun;
I like the slower bells that ring for church
Across the Indiana landscape old.
Therefore I curse the jazz of this hotel
That seems so hot, but is so hard and cold.

DOUGHTRY "DOC" LONG

Black Love Black Hope

[Section 13]

In the middle
of the six o'clock news

or a session with 'Trane
the wind's whistle
on the window
nudges me into
a zero of talk
and I beat my wings
against a closed form
twisting, twisting
flipping, flopping
stacking the rings of dark,
reaching for
an hour ago
when things were horizontal,
but there's no more
watermelon in the ice-box
the kids have torn
the dream book up,
Garvey's birthday
was yesterday,
and the wind keeps
whistling on the window.

[Section 20]

dot and i sipped
ginger brandy
and listened to poems
and short stories
by Coltrane,
street lights
sliced the dark
        polished her and
brought thoughts of
tomorrow and next week
when she'd be gone,
i tried to consume her
she laughed
shy and real
and out beyond Coltrane,
brandy,
street lights and an urgency
junkies in shades
bobbed and weaved talking

black power and
of how hip it was
being hip.

MICHAEL LONGLEY

Words for Jazz Perhaps

for Solly Lipsitz

Elegy for Fats Waller

Lighting up, lest all our hearts should break,
His fiftieth cigarette of the day,
Happy with so many notes at his beck
And call, he sits there taking it away,
The maker of immaculate slapstick.

With music and with such precise rampage
Across the deserts of the blues a trail
He blazes, towards the one true mirage,
Enormous on a nimble-footed camel
And almost refusing to be his age.

He plays for hours on end and though there be
Oases one part water, two parts gin,
He tumbles past to reign, wise and thirsty,
At the still centre of his loud dominion—
THE SHOOK THE SHAKE THE SHEIKH OF ARABY.

Bud Freeman in Belfast

Fog horn and factory siren intercept
Each fragile hoarded-up refrain. What else
Is there to do but let those notes erupt

Until your fading last glissando settles
Among all other sounds—carefully wrapped
In the cotton wool from aspirin bottles?

To Bessie Smith

You bring from Chattanooga Tennessee
Your huge voice to the back of my mind

117

Where, like sea shells salvaged from the sea
As bright reminders of a few weeks' stay,
Some random notes are all I ever find.
I couldn't play your records every day.

I think of Tra-na-rossan, Inisheer,
Of Harris drenched by horizontal rain—
Those landscapes I must visit year by year.
I do not live with sounds so seasonal
Nor set up house for good. Your blues contain
Each longed-for holiday, each terminal.

To Bix Beiderbecke

In hotel rooms, in digs you went to school.
These dead were voices from the floor below
Who filled like an empty room your skull,

Who shared your perpetual one-night stand
—The havoc there, and the manœuvrings!—
Each coloured hero with his instrument.

You were bound with one original theme
To compose in your head your terminus,
Or to improvise with the best of them

That parabola from blues to barrelhouse.

THOMAS LUX

Night above the Town

In the glassed-in jazz club acres above
flat streets spoking distant ovals
I think of: Foster Grandparents. Because,
so many stories below, isolated,
oxygen-starved on asphalt, is a blue
and white Foster Grandparents bus. The tunes
up here are dumb and loud
so I look down
to what I can see: I think
it would be good
to have a foster grandparent, I'll apply

and plead a need for wisdom
and brownies. —Grandma, pinched one,
I want your tin-tasting sharp calm,
come back both grouchy and smart;
Grandfather, distanced,
disinherit me, pass again your cool palms
along the flats of my head . . . I'll apply
tomorrow—if there's a bus
then there's an office
and *slam!* what I'm back to is bad
music, the xylophonist seems to be beating
mice to death, there's a foul
pelican sax and the smell
of youth's pleasant sex and sweat and all
their hundreds of feet on the floor
and fists keeping time
on the tables . . . Grandmother. Grandfather.

NAOMI LONG MADGETT

Echoes

for Duke Ellington

The piano keys sit stiff and stark, sterile
as false teeth in a mouth
that no longer sings,
their black and white notes frozen
into cacophony of loss.

'I let a s-o-n-g go outa-my-heart'
and joy will never mount upon its wings
the same again.

But those perfect stones
tossed into timeless canyons
will reverberate in concentric melody
that will go on
        and on
          and . . . .

Plea for My Heart's Sake

I know you think of me when you are lonely
And only dubious clouds command your sky.
I know that in the silent hush of evening
When shadows fall it is for me you sigh.

I never doubt that, where the rushes thicken
In some lost, God-forsaken wilderness,
A quaint remembrance makes your pulses quicken
And it is my remembrance that you bless.

But in the city's turbulent obsession,
Blind in the glaring lights, deaf in the scream
Of jazz refrains and dancers gaily swaying,
Will you forget me and the white moon's gleam?

When you come back to lights and wine and music,
I beg you not to need me any less,
For if you love me in your silent sorrow,
Then love me also in your happiness.

HAKI MADHUBUTI

Don't Cry, Scream

for John Coltrane/ from a black poet/
in a basement apt. crying dry tears
of "you ain't gone."

into the sixties
a trane
came/ out of the
fifties with a
golden boxcar
riding the rails
of novation.
        blowing
        a–melodics
        screeching,

screaming,
blasting—
              driving some away,
              (those paper readers who thought
              manhood was something innate)

              bring others in,
              (the few who didn't believe that the
              world existed around established whi
              teness & leonard bernstein)
music that ached.
murdered our minds (we reborn)
born into a neoteric aberration.
& suddenly
you envy the
BLIND man—
you know that he will
hear what you'll never
see.
              your music is like
              my head—nappy black/
              a good nasty feel with
              tangled songs of:
                    we-eeeeeeeeee   sing
                    WE-EEEeeeeeeeeee   loud &
                    WE-EEEEEEEEEEEEEEEE   high
                                              with
                                              feeling

a people playing
the sound of me when
i combed it. combed at
it.

i cried for billie holiday.
the blues. we ain't blue
the blues exhibited illusions of manhood.
destroyed by you. Ascension into:

              scream-eeeeeeeeeeeeee-ing   sing
              SCREAM-EEEeeeeeeeeeee-ing   loud &
              SCREAM-EEEEEEEEEEEEEEE-ing   long with
                                              feeling

we ain't blue, we are black.
we ain't blue, we are black.
                (all the blues did was
                make me cry)
soultrane gone on a trip
he left man images
he was a life-style of
man-makers & annihilator
of attache case carriers.

Trane done went.
(got his hat & left me one)
naw brother,
i didn't cry,
i just—

    Scream-eeeeeeeeeeeeeee-ed   sing loud
    SCREAM-EEEEEEEEEEEEEEEEEEE-ED   & high with
     we-eeeeeeeeeeeeeeeeeeeeee ee   feeling
    WE-EEEEEEeeeeeeeeeEEEEEEEE   letting
    WE-EEEEEEEEEEEEEEEEEEEEEEE   yr/voice
    WHERE YOU DONE GONE, BROTHER? break

it hurts, grown babies
dying. born. done caught me
a trane. steel wheels broken
by popsicle sticks. i went out
& tried to buy a nickel bag
with my standard oil card.

blonds had more fun—
with snagga-tooth niggers
who saved pennies & pop bottles for week-ends
to play negro & other filthy inventions.
be-bop-en to james brown's
cold sweat—these niggers didn't sweat,
they perspired. & the blond's dye came out,
i ran. she did too, with his pennies, pop bottles
& his mind. tune in next week same time same station
for anti-self in one lesson.

to the negro cow-sissies
who did tchaikovsky &
the beatles & live in

split-level homes & had
split-level minds & babies.
who committed the act of
love with their clothes on.

>(who hid in the bathroom to read
>jet mag., who didn't read the chicago
>defender because of the misspelled
>words & had shelves of books by
>europeans on display. untouched. who
>hid their little richard & lightnin'
>slim records & asked: "John who?"

>instant hate.)

they didn't know any better,
brother, they were too busy getting
into debt, expressing humanity &
taking off color.

>SCREAMMMM/we-eeeee/screech/teee improvise
>aheeeeeeeee/screeeeeee/theeee/ee with
>ahHHHHHHHHH/WEEEEEEEE/scrEEE feeling
>   EEEE
>we-eeeeeWE-EEEEEEEEWE-EE-EEEEE

the ofays heard you &
were wiped out. spaced.
one clown asked me during,
my favorite things, if
you were practicing.
i fired on the muthafucka & said,
"i'm practicing."

naw brother,
i didn't cry.
i got high off my thoughts—
they kept coming back,
back to destroy me.

& that BLIND man
i don't envy him anymore
i can see his hear
& hear his heard through my pores.
i can see my me. it was truth you gave,
like a daily shit
it had to come.

123

can you scream—brother?   very
can you scream—brother?   soft

i hear you.
i hear you.

and the Gods will too.

Knocking Donkey Fleas off a
Poet from the Southside of Chi

for brother Ted Joans

a worldman.
with the careful eye; the deep look, the newest look.
as recent & hip as the uncola being sipped by
thelonious monk
jackie-ing it down to little *rootie tootie's.*

he's a continent jumper,
a show-upper, a neo-be-bopper.
he's the first u see the last to flee,
the homeboy in African land;
with an inner compass of the rightway.
at times he's the overlooked   like
a rhinoceros in a bird bath.

the sound of his trumpet is the true *off minor.*
to hear him tell it: *bird* is alive, blacks must colonize europe,
          jazz is a woman & I did, I was, I am.
& I believe him.

he's younger than his poems
& old as his clothes,
he's badder than bad: him so bad he cd take a banana from a
          gorilla, pull a pork chop out of a lion's
          buttocks   or debate the horrors of
          war with spiro agnew with his mouth
          closed.
a worldman,
a man of his world.

124

ted joans is the tan of the sun; the sun's tan.
a violent/ peace
looking for a piece.
he'll find it   (in the only place he hasn't been)

among the stars,   that star.
the one that's missing.
last seen
walking slowly across Africa
bringing the rest of the world with it.

RICK MADIGAN

Curtis Fuller

On my fourteenth birthday
when I wanted Stones or Beatles,
Aftermath, Revolver, out of our heads,
which I'd listen to full volume
as I did my trig or algebra,
the disappointing cover said *soul stream trombone*
and showed a man in cap and shades,
the awkward looking horn brought to his lips.
Even so, I told my uncle I *liked* his gift,
then I played it once or twice before
filing it away at the rear of my thick stack
of British Invasion LPs,
and somewhere in some universe
of lost and precious things
that record's still holding its own,
waiting for some callow kid to drop it on the spindle.
My uncle, Jack, might be there too,
dead now almost ten years,
if there exists a heaven for alcoholic know-it-alls,
wife-beaters, jazz freaks, gourmet cooks,
Dartmouth grads and wizard engineers
too arrogant to keep a job for long,
since he was all of those and also was my favorite
talking jazz on his infrequent visits,
razzing me about the rock 'n roll I preferred,
his good music like his good cigar

wafting over my head,
strong opinions on any mentioned subject
no one but my father dared counter,
since no one else could argue quite like Jack
and certainly not my mother who thoroughly despised him,
which he knew but pretended not to notice.
It's the bubble of the spirit bobbing
through notched lines, wavering, holding on,
when someone who's mastered it plays
a slide trombone, the miracle of disaster continuously averted,
that fall down a set of steep barroom stairs
some friendly hand reaching out suspends.
When I heard that Jack had died in a mangrove swamp
alone, pulled over to the shoulder
on his way back to Miami, I put on
Blue Mitchell's Big Six with Curtis Fuller,
and listened to the chases on "Sir John."
At Jack's request his ashes were sprinkled
from a plane, friends chugging low over the Gulf,
sunny day in Lauderdale, Jack fanned to the clouds,
his same friends in flowered shirts
who had commandeered the funeral,
danced with my mother,
slapped my father on the back,
then took my favorite uncle in his urn.

Stereo Time with Booker Little

One time in the middle of "Goin' Down Slow"
Miss Nude California slipped her hands inside his pants
and he still didn't fuck up the song,
though he was competent, that's all,
on the Telecaster bass
he knew well enough to know what not to play,
how to stay untangled from piano and guitar
while the band stayed crucially alert,
one eye always watchful on the crowd,
so as not to get nailed with a bottle.
They worked five sets a night in the local topless bar
trying hard, God knows why, to please that room,
though it hardly mattered what they would

or wouldn't do—gaudy stage in front of them
across that cave-like, black-light tomb,
dancers turning zombie-like undressing in the dark,
they played to the backs of rough mens' heads.
But the music meant almost everything then
is all he wants to say,
to anyone who's kind enough to listen,
even more than those few young women he knew
who'd brave that place to hear them,
since in truth even they did not go there for music.
In Bill Nye's trailer where he sometimes
also slept, they'd practice till Nye's neighbors
threw rocks against the wall
and the whole room shook like a cracked and beaten drum,
or until cold fingers cramped and bled.
What he learned was how to listen
which he now does more than ever
to the soundtrack each clear morning brings,
today Booker Little, trumpeter supreme,
twenty-two years old and turning what comes in his head
forwards and backwards, upside down,
the kind of dervish motion, intelligence and grace,
he wouldn't find if he played a thousand years.
At only 23 Little dies of uremia,
toxins in the blood and the kidneys shutting down,
leaving just a few albums of his own
plus a couple with Dolphy, Roach, and Coltrane—
all of it together not nearly enough
for the elegiac music bursting from his embouchure,
fully-formed already, gray-eyed and serene,
ready even for the heartless world,
as if Booker Little from Memphis, Tennessee,
knew and understood his fate.
The disc that's on today was cut in 1960
when stereo was still almost new,
separation so clear he can feel the open spaces
crackling past the band,
half-a-dozen steps across the rented Jersey studio
as if he were a presence in that room,
one sweet breath that's pressed through time
which is nothing, an echo or a spell.
He can look up from his chair and witness

Little come alive, one moment of reflection
before he razors in and the screen of deep blue night
snaps down, Wynton Kelly on piano
across that humming system
and Roy Haynes in full glide above the drums.

WILLIAM MATTHEWS

The Buddy Bolden Cylinder

It doesn't exist, I know, but I love
to think of it, wrapped in a shawl
or bridal veil, or, less dramatically,
in an old copy of the *Daily Picayune*,
and like an unstaled, unhatched egg
from which, at the right touch, like mine,
the legendary tone, sealed these long years
in the amber of neglect, would peal and re-
peal across the waters. What waters do
I have in mind? Nothing symbolic, mind you.
I meant the sinuous and filth-rich
Mississippi across which you could hear
him play from Gretna, his tone was so loud
and sweet, with a moan in it like you were
in church, and on those old, slow, low-down
blues Buddy could make the women jump
the way they liked. But it doesn't exist,
it never did, except as a relic
for a jazz hagiography, and all
we think we know about Bolden's music
is, really, a melancholy gossip
and none of it sown by Bolden, who
spent his last twenty-four years in Jackson
(Insane Asylum of Louisiana)
hearing the voices of people who spooked
him before he got there. There's more than one
kind of ghostly music in the air, all
of them like the wind: you can't see it
but you can see the leaves shiver in place
as if they'd like to turn their insides out.

Mingus at the Showplace

I was miserable, of course, for I was seventeen,
and so I swung into action and wrote a poem,

and it was miserable, for that was how I thought
poetry worked: you digested experience and shat

literature. It was 1960 at The Showplace, long since
defunct, on West 4th St., and I sat at the bar,

casting beer money from a thin reel of ones,
the kid in the city, big ears like a puppy.

And I knew Mingus was a genius. I knew two
other things but they were wrong, as it happened.

So I made him look at the poem.
"There's a lot of that going around," he said,

and Sweet Baby Jesus he was right. He laughed
amiably. He didn't look as if he thought

bad poems were dangerous, the way some poets do.
If they were baseball executives they'd plot

to destroy sandlots everywhere so that the game
could be saved from children. Of course later

that night he fired his pianist in mid-number
and flurried him from the stand.

"We've suffered a diminuendo in personnel,"
he explained, and the band played on.

KENNETH MAY

Valentine's Day

Charlie Parker's on the off ramp
driving a convertible he borrowed

from a friend, & Billie's
suspended in the vinyl, her voice

next for the needle. Tonight, I leave
dope alone & go for a walk

after neighbors close their curtains,
switch off the lights. Stars

lean from behind clouds the way a child
looks around a corner. I think about

Woman at Point Zero who said
killing is sometimes gentle.

Along the Rio Grande, war planes'
sonic booms punch holes in the sky

& collapse adobe homes like falling
in sleep. She's a mirage

in a far off galaxy of numbers. I come
upon a stalled train & want to ride

back to last autumn, forget that she's in
a different area code. Heaven

for those who need help, I'm chained to
the front door as Bird meanders

on alto. I picture her walking
the Brooklyn Bridge, Lorca's Spanish verses

a thunderstorm on her lips. A good
American rose should last at least a week.

MICHAEL MCCLURE

For Monk

ALL IS COOL AND BOUNDLESS AS A ROLLING
LAMB OF JAZZ, I SEE
the shades slipped behind me. Avolekitesvara!
I am blessed and protected. I hear the beauty
of the tossing notes. I am safe!
I — it does not matter — love Avolekitesvara, Kwannon,
love you pale beauty.
See my twisted head and face grow
thin again.
PURSUE THE SLIM SHADES IN AND OUT
LOST IN IT ALL,

and hide you from myself, choke
on my love for you, happy
for an instant.

(All is fire and I fat myself to be a candle.)

(Careful, careful crazy man and burning heart.)

OH! OH! OH! OH! Tired old fear. OH! OH!

THOMAS MCGRATH

Guiffre's Nightmusic

There is moonrise under your fingernail—
Light broken from a black stick
Where your hands in darkness are sorting the probables.

Hunger condenses midnight on the tongue . . .
Journeys . . . Blues . . . ladder of slow bells,
Toward the cold hour of lunar prophecy:

A scale-model city, unlighted, in a shelf
In the knee of the Madonna; a barbwire fence
Strummed by the wind: dream-singing emblems.

—The flags that fly above the breakfast food
    Are not your colors.
                    The republic of the moon
    Gives no sleepy medals. Nor loud ornament.

Jazz at the Intergalactic Nightclub

The management is pleased to announce:
That as a result of the recent elections to the Universal
                    Congress of Transmogrification,
There will be revelations . . . visions . . . charismatic hors-
            d'heuvres . . . mana . . . divine grace . . .
Exactly at midnight;

And is further pleased to advise you
That every instant of time this bright dark long,
No matter what the time-belt of your home province,

Shall be that true and enduring midnight,
This eternal heaven in which we dream of hell.

Look at the clock, ladies and gentlemen:
It is three seconds until that ultimate midnight,
That Universal Prime, moment of Grace, final rent payment,
                              Revelation, Satori,

Three . . .
Two . . .
One . . .

There.
It has happened.

Now you may all go home.

JAMES MCKEAN

After Listening to Jack Teagarden . . .

I will blame him,
the man who convinced my mother
there was talent in long arms,
whose baton held me lock-stepped
all summer in three songs,
who never revealed the old name
for trombone is sackbut,
as awkward as the black vinyl case
I banged against my knees
in a neighborhood where salvation
meant running. *Sackbut,*
the first girl I ever kissed,
wet-mouthed and blowing
and not a sound, much less a sob
of music. I blame him
for one lost summer, my mouth full of oil,
stuck spit valves, the slide
dented over and over by the ground.
Yes, him, for my bird-flushing,
window-rattling squawks,
for the anonymous gift of a mute,
for my memory of him yet
like the music stand I could never fold

right again. May he hear me
once more in the Lake City parade,
timed by his whistle,
all oxfords and a new white shirt.
May he forgive my faking
the two songs I never learned.
May he accept the blame
for my marching out of step up the rear
of the Ridgecrest Mounted Posse,
their horses farting
as I lost myself in "Sweet Georgia Brown,"
the only song I remembered
as loud as I could.

SANDRA MCPHERSON

The Ability to Make a Face Like a Spider While Singing Blues: Junior Wells

Who knows if they sing in their webs
or while hunting—they may never have tried
their voices, and what is a spider throat?
But until we know that, a singer thinking
about a *mean black spider* becomes one
without thinking and intends to race
the winged ones through the stickiest place.
Cock your head; when you squint, the
light will throw you reasonable prey,
what you deserve, a gleam, a solo look,
a song to repair the break of day.

Some Metaphysics of Junior Wells

18 September 1987

1

A night universe scallop-edged with his faces—
surprise mostly—one shock unmasking another,
one, out of still water, splashing another.

Astonishment, as if a bird had landed on his head.

Amazement stronger than awe, more aggressive than awe.

A day universe? "Promoters pissing on your head,
trying to make you believe it's raining."

2

He says he's been "fucking up the whole tour"—everyone's
mad at him; but tonight he is thrilled to feel
as well as he does.

The dusk, his partner thinks, is Southern:
"The mosquitos bring the air."
Full moon, farmland, horse, and goat.
Junior is as light

as three nighthawks.
     Singing with his arms,
he migrates, assuming the wind-brushed form
for aerial carriage.

3

He washes his hands
around his harp;
fist hits his heart,
shoots out one long finger.
He looks into one hand,
counts with it, waves,
trills it, it curves like grass,
it signals *Stop*.
One hand is quick on hip,
waggles, clicks; thumbs up,
hand shakes off time,
thumb rolls in and out of fist.
One hand folds in over harp.
A cormorant's wing. Index
makes a #1. He boxes.
One hand flashes, plays
his waist; he shaves
with a hand's edge.
Claps heels of palms, a fist
is something to release; fingertips
kiss his mouth; hand
makes a sign like water.

4

You can make a sound bigger than yourself.
You can sign a sound bigger than yourself.
You can whirl sound around in your mouth.

You can make a music which is only your face in silence.

You can squint your lips and *clock* your tongue.
You can hoot and melodize.
You can never waste a thing.

In right creation there is no waste.
(But the hours before, the living between?)
None. You can add matter to the universe.

In the wind the bird saw several faces.
They were all different, easy to tell apart.
They were Beginning, Birth, Newness, and Dawn.

Suspension: Junior Wells on a Small Stage in a Converted Barn

As the phobic said: it is torture
to leave the land, to feel distance
between bridge-body and bay-water.
And the way she feels in that slow crowded lane

a listener feels hearing the falling-space
from a voice's full clothing to its thin bones
although his harp is cables
wavering and secure.

Early set tied tight. Late set—the audience shifts, baffled
with his fun: a long disassembly
of bars, and then he rides a sideman,
forces music out of others younger,

forces trouble up and out of consolation.
He tears a note, makes rags of others,
uses them to shine the sound waves
at the far end of the bridge.

"We cannot experience that storied head
in which Apollo's eyeballs ripened like . . ."—

135

like what?—is it honor, accuracy,
not to finish it? Don't sentence? How

the smallest gesture, little
backpedaling dance or yowl,
is distilled from all the crushed. Like cider.
Like apple-scent. Then sweet courtesy:

"May I say something?" Then the howl.
The little yodel that hovers,
black-throated sparrow, easy in its own extremes,
not knowing whether to land

by the person begging its winter ground
with seeds. It is followed
by grinding, a good groan,
and phrasing low but on toes,

like the farm cat snooping in the bass drum hoop.
And then remorse—
a scrapping of takes, though each began
with leap and bite.

It is not fear or distance that incompletes his songs,
vaporizes them mid-melisma:
song is denied its beautiful death, its resolution,
yet I'm left with resolve—

deny endings to any song, I'll hold the threads.
To yourself you are always live,
but an audience terminated
by show-end and song-end

is falsely complete: the voice-search goes on,
you show them, sounding out
beginnings and middles tonight, the fertile middle
of the night. No last dawn-azure word.

You can't stop singing,
pure gist, suspension. Your holdings,
a sung estate of fragments, remain unabridged.
And you'll be incomplete but never still,

abandoning in favor, in favor of, always.
This is how it must be to make a language,
hands filling out phrases,
silences

each one different from the next. . . .

But of course he was accused,

of sampling. Of tasting a song and putting it back.

And these fragments flew him over the plank walk   over the mud
to his dressing room   the way birds (sparrows after the thaw
—a pair of Old World house sparrows
yesterday in a city gas station   on an aberrant
rescindably warm February noon   almost all the snow
melted except that plowed into piles and iced)   the way birds
pick up from a gutter a straw   a piece of cigarette pack
cellophane   a blade of grass and fly it to   their unfinished nest

DAVID MELTZER

17:II:82

Thelonious Monk dies
today my 45th birth
day
years ago
a Seattle dj
told me this story:

Thelonious was playing here
with the Giants of Jazz group
dodged all requests for interviews
but I got through somehow & found him
in his hotelroom laying down
w/ a pace-maker on his chest
his silence unhinged me
but I kept talking
& after a while
he'd say something
nothing really
a grunt
& I asked him
what it was that he did
I mean
what he thought when he played

some dumb thing like that
like what he thought his music did
Monk didn't answer
he kept looking at a second-hand
circle the electric clockface
on the dresser
then looked at me & said
"I put it down.
You got to pick it up."

18:VI:82

for Art Pepper

Paul's *niemandsrose*
I place in Art's brass bell
alto Selmer on its stand

despite
encyclopedic light
held & shattered
by its curves
the horn's silent

& the rose
white like paper

ADRIAN MITCHELL

From Rich Uneasy America to My Friend Christopher Logue

'Never again that sick feeling when the toilet overflows.'
advertisement: The Iowa City Press–Citizen.

Jim Hall's guitar walking around
As if the Half Note's wooden floor
Grew blue flowers and each flower
Drank from affluent meadow ground.
The lush in the corner dropped his sorrowing

When he noticed his hands and elbows dancing.
Long silver trucks made lightning past the window.
A two-foot hunter watch hung from the ceiling.
Then you prowled in. The guitar splintered,
The lush held hands with himself, trucks concertinaed.
The watch-hands shook between Too Late and Now.

As I sit easy in the centre
Of the U.S. of America,
Seduced by cheeseburgers, feeling strong
When bourbon licks my lips and tongue,
Ears stopped with jazz or both my eyes
Full of Mid-Western butterflies,
You drive out of a supermarket
With petrol bombs in a family packet
And broadcast down your sickened nose:
'It overflows. By Christ, it overflows.'

ERNST MOERMAN

Louis Armstrong

(translated from the French by Samuel Beckett)

suddenly in the midst of a game of lotto with his sisters
Armstrong let a roar out of him that he had the raw meat
red wet flesh for Louis
and he up and he sliced him two rumplips
since when his trumpet bubbles
their fust buss

poppies burn on the black earth
he weds the flood he lulls her

some of these days muffled in ooze
down down down down
pang of white in my hair

after you're gone
Narcissus lean and slippered

you're driving me crazy and the trumpet
is Ole Bull it chassés aghast
out of the throes of morning

down the giddy catgut
and *confessing* and my woe slavers
the black music it can't be easy
it threshes the old heart into a spin
into a blaze

Louis lil' ole fader Mississippi
his voice gushes into the lake
the rain spouts back into heaven
his arrows from afar they fizz through the wild horses
they fang you and me
then they fly home

flurry of lightning in the earth
sockets for his rootbound song
nights of Harlem scored with his nails
snow black slush when his heart rises

his she-notes they have more tentacles than the sea
they woo me they close my eyes
they suck me out of the world

AMUS MOR

The Coming of John

(the evening and the morning were the first day)

it is friday
the eagle has flown
4 years before the real god Allah shows
before we know the happenings
we eat the devils' peck
mondays hotlinks with porkenbeans
hear "newk" on dig and "bags" on moonray
see desolation in the dark between the buildings
our front view is bricks of the adjacent kitchenette

Pat riffs in a babyfied key
slips on the green knit suit
with the silver buckle at the belly
and we slide out into that wintertime
the last lights of day

with an uncanny clarity for chi town
the shafts behind the clouds popping them open
and the rust on the el grids
clashing and blending strangely
against the rays like hip black art

heaven about to show itself
above the ghetto holiday shoppers
the 1954 brand fragments of people on the walks
hadacol on her way north
after officer driseldorf has stomped her on the street
and crushed her finger on a golden ring

the hipster in the tivoli eat shop
deals single joints after the commotion
dusk baring his first meal
with us steaming and talking about the guns
getting so mad and so frantic we sweat
get on to cool
go on home
make love and nod
then it is the new year
and the guns are going off across the alley

10 days or so hes still "on this end"
only Edwardo Harris knowing his name
John Coltrane (as he was called then)
in a big hat
gouster pleated pants and all
before metamorphosis miles plugs cotton in his ears
and philadelphia thunders in babylon
a shake dancer follows the set
and it seems a whole sea of black faces are out on "six trey"
a holy nation peeping and poor
behind the red oblong bulb of a highlife sign

Ohnedaruth the mystic has already blown and hypnotized
                                                    us—

making us realize right then
THAT WE ARE LIVING IN THE BIBLE (HOLY KORAN, CABALA)

the kenatechi girl sits there frozen
shes followed her lifelong scent of judea
from the rich north shore township

141

all the way into the crown propeller lounge
into a blessed tenors bell
while we go "off into space"
peeping the dream of the old ladies of nipon
dragging the bags of brown smack across the dead
                                        battlefields
chanting "fun amelikaan" "fun amelikaan" "fun joo"

"All right, na iss a party. Ya dig that. Na Miles come and be doin all la
rights thangs ya understand. Take the hordevures from the lazy susan with
so much finese. An be so correct when when he be talking to them big
fine socialite Hos. They be sayin 'Oh Miles', understand.

"Na here come Trane. He wrong from the get go Reach his hand down
in the tray. Say 'gimme one of them little samaches'. He done pushed the
pushed the mop out the way, took the jonny walker red way from one of
the Ivy league dames and drank it down out the bottle. An Miles see he
diggin him. He his man, he brought the man in here for that. They
working together, understand.

"What the man is tryin ta tell ya wit his horn, is that you all can't get
nowhere being what the bray call intell gent. If yall want to get some-
where in america, ya gotta start bustin down dos and shit. Knocking these
lames upside the head. Pitchin a fit. Laying these peckerwoods out cross
the room is whas go getchu somewhere in america. Now if y'all don't
start, letting yall's wigs grown wild and shit and start gettin' all up in greys
faces, just like me and like mau maus. Africa an sixty third street ain't no
different. Y'all ain't going another futher, understand. Because this shit in
this country richere, is all comin down to some head bustin'." Sho anuff.

we stay till the lights
pull the covers off the room
showing the ragged carpet
in the great american tradition
(mayhap a manager)
make in in
fire up two thumbs and sleep
t.i. on a pallet in front of the bad window

and the hotel catches fire
the lobbys all smoking
the few steel workers with their helmets
the several a.d.c. families

the pimps, the hustlers and the chippies
are all milling around out of it
when the "konat girl" turns up in smoke
in just leotards and a mouton coat
now shes took the pressing iron to her slavic hair
(that morning is the second day)

LARRY NEAL

Don't Say Goodbye to the Pork-Pie Hat

for Langston Hughes

Don't say goodbye to the pork-pie hat that rolled along on
    padded shoulders,
                    that swang be-hop phrases
                    in Minton's jelly-roll dreams.
don't say goodbye to hip hats tilted in the style of a soulful era,
the pork-pie hat that Lester dug,
swirling in the sound of sun saxes,
repeating phrase on phrase, repeating bluely
as hi-hat cymbals crash and trumpets scream while
musicians move in and out of this gloom; the pork-pie hat
    reigns supreme,
the elegance of style
gleaned from the city's underbelly.
                    tonal memories
                    tonal memories
of salt-peanuts and hot house birds. the pork-pie hat
                                    sees.
And who was the musician who
            blew Bird way by accident, then died, obscure,
an obscene riff repeating lynch scenes?
repeating weird changes. The chorus repeats itself also, the
    horns slide
from note to note in blue, in blue streaks of mad wisdom;
blues notes
coiling around

the pork-pie hat and the drum-dancing hips defying the
    sanctity of white
America.
and who was the trumpet player in that small town in Kansas
    who
        begged to sit in,
blew a chorus, then fainted dead on the bandstand?
blew you away.
that same musician resurrected himself in Philly at the Blue
    Note Cafe
                        Ridge Avenue and 16th St.
after the third set, had him an old horn and was wearing the
    pork-pie
                        hat.
wasn't he familiar? didn't you think that you were seeing a
        ghost?
and didn't the pork-pie hat leave Minton's
                        for 52nd St.?
and didn't it later make it to Paris where they dug him too?
and didn't the pork-pie buy Bird a meal in '35
when said musician was kicked out of the High-Hat (18th &
    South)
                                for blowing

strange changes?

I saw the pork-pie hat skimming the horizon
                        flashing bluegreenyellowlights
he was blowing black stars
and
weird looneymoon changes and chords were wrapped around
    him
                                    and he was flying
fast, zipping past note, past sound into cosmic silence.
Caresses flowed from the voice in the horn in the blue
of the yellow whiskey room where hustlers
with big coats and fly sisters moved; finger popping while
            tearing at chicken and waffles—
the pork-pie hat loomed specter like, a vision for the world,
dressed in a camel hair coat, shiny knob toe shoes, sporting
a hip pin stripe suit with pants pressed razor sharp, caressing
    his horn
        baby-like.

And who was the bitch in the bar in Boston who kept trying
    to make it
with the pork-pie hat while it fingered for the changes
on Dewey Square? She almost make you blow your cool.
you did blow your cool, 'cause on the side I got you hollered
shut-up across that slick white boy's
tape recorder. Yeah the one who copped your music & made
some fat money after you died. didn't you
                          blow your cool?
and didn't you almost lose your pork-pie hat behind all that
    shit?
Who was the ofay chick that followed the group
                    from Boston to Philly
                    from New York to Washington
                    from Chicago to Kansas City
                    was that Backstage Sally?
or was Backstage Sally a blue-voiced soul sister who lived
                              on Brown street in Philly.
who dug you, who fed you cold nights with soul food
and soul-body. was that Backstage Sally?
Sounds drift above the cities of Black America;
all over America black musicians are putting
on the pork-pie hat again, picking up their axes,
preparing to blow away the white dream. you can
hear them screeching love in rolling sheets of sound;
with movement and rhythm recreating themselves and the
    world;
sounds splintering the deepest regions of the spiritual
    universe—
crisp and moaning voices leaping in the horns of destruction,
blowing doom and death to all who have no use for the Spirit.
don't say goodbye to the pork-pie hat, it lives. Yeah . . .

Lester lives and leaps
Delancey's dilemma is over
Bird lives
Lady lives
Eric stands next to me
while I finger the afro-horn
Bird lives
Lady lives
Lester leaps in every night

Tad's delight
is mine now
Dinah knows
Fats and Wardell blow fours
Dinah knows
Richie knows
that Bud is Buddha
that Bird is Shango
that Jelly Roll dug ju-ju
and Lester lives
in Ornette's leaping
the blues live
we live. live
spirit lives. the sound
lives bluebirdlives
lives and leaps. dig
the bluevoices
dig the pork pie dig
the spirit in Sun Ra's sound. dig
spirit lives in sound
lives sound spirit
sound lives in spirit
spirit lives in sound. blow.
spirit lives
spirit lives
spirit lives
SPIRIT . . . . . ! ! ! ! . . . . . SWHEEEEEET ! ! ! !
   Take it
      again, this time from the chorus

Lady's Days

More song. birds follow the sun.
rain comes . . .
we drive South, me and Billie
rain.

Was it D.C.; or the hick towns
of square yokels come to hear the Lady sing?

Rain. these nights on the road, the car, these
towns lingering blue in her voice.

146

South where birds go.
I remember them faces
the soft and the hard
faces scarred, wailing
for the song and the moan
digging the gardenia thing
she was into . . .

Lady's days

Digging the song as it turned soft
in her mouth
digging as the mouth turned softly
in the song . . .
They dug you, yeah
heavy smoke moaning
room shifting under red spotlights
And then there was the Philly bust.
Hey now lover, you said, don't worry . . .
some towns are like that . . . But the music
is somewhere else . . .

Those were copacetic times, eh Mama?
Down the hall, morning rises bright
and weird in Lester's horn.
We watch the sun scat over the river
and then our bodies merge into his song.

Lady's days

Now rain
on the road again, rain.
Herbie is driving
you sleep, pressed against my chest . . .
I can still hear Prez's solo
from last night's gig . . .
the light dreams
the warm woman in my arms
and her mellow voice hovering over us . . .
My woman
Billie beautiful
My woman, Lady Day

child of the God of Song . . .
heavy smell of alcohol and moan
spotlights for the Lady
raining gardenias and blues.

Faces. the pain rides them
more pain
their pain
ghosts ride them
your voice rides them
shifting under red spotlights . . .
smoke.

One night between sets, I asked you what it meant.
the pain raining
and the moans of scars and gardenias.
I had just finished running some scales
in quiet sixteenths when I asked you:
Is that the way it is Billie baby?
I recall you humming a line from
one of my solos
and then you laughed, that real pretty laugh.
Slow power of the blues, you said.
you said, you said that it had to go
down that way; honey, ain't gotta be no
reason for towns, faces, moans . . .

MWATABU OKANTAH

Afreeka Brass

i hear you Trane,
sounding that mountain,
touched by age-old
"Alabama" pain.

inside my inner ear
brass elephants
trumpeting Elvin's
stampeding cymbal'd lion
roar.

with you Trane;
rumbling "Song of the
Underground Railroad" movering
my blood, keeping
our born-into heart
beat alive,
regal,
and black . . .

Africa

Southern Road

for Sterling A. Brown
(1901–1989)

you walked dusty dry roads;
No Hidin' Place.
you refused patrons.
you back-turned confusion
in bath tub gin;

down home poeming
Slim Greer of us,
melodic sneer of us,
"strong men git stronger" of us,

you remembered Ma Rainey of us.
you word-magic'd our need
for Bessie's moan (yes, still this po'
inch worm "keep a-inchin' along").

you braved rock white roads
ballad bluesing
our Caravan
blood.

you walked stoney why roads;
that Southern Road.
we can now know
our real strength
is in brown love . . .

RON OVERTON

Blues in "C"

in memory: Gil Evans (1912–1988)

1.
It's the torque of a spring Sunday
wound against the eardrum, the first open window
letting outside in, late afternoon,
already the temperature beginning to dip,
the ferry heading out
sounding its pompous horn (though there is no fog,
just these late chords of light),
then answered
by the train rocking toward Port Jeff,
all the disparate sounds an uneasy harmony:
snarl of dirtbikes and power saws, motorcycles
showing off winding through their gears,
the yip of a mutt, swoosh of a convertible that leaves
in its wake dead leaves swirling among green buds,
and the blips of a video game take their place too,
as natural as the two crows outside the window
mocking in rough counterpoint,
or the voices
inside houses down the block, dim and pleading,
families reprising their sad histories. . . .

2.
And I think of your late band, the dense variety
of sounds overlapping, stopping, starting, waiting,
the loose rhythms washing against one another,
moody and tidal,
nothing urgent to be resolved,
notes milling, out on a limb—
wisecracks, potshots, pratfalls—
then the wild facts gathered, shuffled, swung
into jet stream riffs above drum cauldrons
till precipitation! Hot rain of notes, sleet squalls,
then a shiver of alto joy down the spine of sorrow—

always up to the edge, whelming, striving,
then moving on,
a new timbre, shifting ground,
a lush dissonance bending toward a harmony,
as the sun goes, as *Blues in "C"* quiets finally,
like two friends tired of quarreling,
like the hush after testimony,
after desire . . .
Parabola life!

New song to the end!
The older you got, the younger it got.
The window thrust open,
song letting everything in . . .

3.
every day something happens
that's not supposed to happen
that's not on the calendar
not in the cards

it's the body breaking down
it's the boy in the well
too many ambulances in the bays
the window sealed by paint

sometimes I feel
like a mother of the pedestrian
no invention in sight
                              then the maya
of neon on rainy streets
the crackle of a flung shirt and
the electricity is back
                              even
the fictionist of sorrow
with the cult who adores his silence
begins to speak
                      the musician
who lays the horn down
to catch his breath
and waits five years
picks it up and sings
                          a blues

151

so ardent the notes so true
they make you smile
(in a parenthesis of pain)
the smile of consent

4.
The whisper of sprinklers has stopped,
water eddies along the curb, it's laced with soap bubbles
(the humming carwashers have gone inside)
in whose sheen
are reflected the white clouds
and the blue heavens imperceptibly turning darker,
darker: and it is quiet now.

And it is quieter now.

RAYMOND R. PATTERSON

Hopping Toad Blues

What I give that man, some other woman takes.
Everything I give that man, some other woman takes.
It don't do no good to fatten frogs for snakes.

Some bullfrogs, they got double-jointed knees.
Some bullfrogs they got double-jointed knees,
Like to hop around anywhere they please.

Hangs out all night, says he's just catching flies.
He's out all night, says he's just catching flies,
Comes hopping home, big rings around his eyes.

Hopping toad, you gonna muddy up your pond.
You swim in muddy water, you gonna muddy up your pond—
Come hopping home one morning and find your sweet mama gone.

Sundown Blues

Sun going down,
I won't see this day again.
Sun going down,
Sure won't see this day again.
When I started out,
I didn't think this day would end.

I saw a face in my mirror
And didn't know that face was mine.
A face in my mirror,
And didn't know that face was mine.
If you meet a stranger
Sometimes it pays to be kind.

Folks try to live,
They don't always live right.
Folks just trying to live,
They don't always live right.
When day is done
Ain't nothing left but night.

Sun going down,
Won't see this day again.
Sun going down,
Won't see this day again.
When I started out,
I didn't think this day would end.

USENI EUGENE PERKINS

Boss Guitar

for Wes Montgomery

Charlie (Christian) died
even younger . . . but you
knew about his legacy anyway.
It showed in your chords
Those beautiful chords you played so well.

Chords that bounced around
like black women dancing
to African rhythms.
Chords that others tried
to imitate but became
frustrated from lack of
technique that comes from
plucking strings without a
                              pick.

They were still talking about
Django Reinhardt until you blew
on the scene. (then the memory
                    of the gypsy died
                    like everything else
                    that becomes numb from
                    too much pain)

You could do it all
Inspire other musicians to
Break sound barriers/
Invent harmonies (that moved)
show what Duke meant when
he talked about swing/or feel
                    like Lady Day when
                    she sung the blues
                    about those sad
                    evenings she left
                    in Harlem.

White people use to laugh
at black banjo players/and
praise Arthur Godfrey for
playing a ukelele. but the string
                    has always been
                    our thing.

Remember those Blues players who
could make a twelve string guitar
play chords that weren't even on
                    the charts.

Beautiful chords like you played so well
Boss chords coming from a BOSS GUITAR
Charlie would've dug your style
you both had so much in common.

fluent moves/drive/soul/and of
course these beautiful chords
you played so well.

Jazz Poem

Dead musicians are not jazz lovers
even those who were buried to the
                              funeral marches of
                              Rev. J. M. Gates
                         When Charlie Christian
died he left his guitar to be envied
by classical faggots with Ph.D.
                                   certificates.
White imitators tried to claim Ragtime
until Scott Joplin put them in
                                   their graves.
The stride pianos of Jimmy Yancey and
Meade Lux Lewis kept the prohibition era
from becoming a complete drag.
And Benny Goodman advocates used to
                         sneak into Mintons
                         with propaganda about
                         Paul Whiteman starting
                         a new jazz movement.
While the Bean and Sidney Bechet
took an exodus to France
                         seeking Parisian wine
                         and economic survival.
Fats Waller and
Fletcher Henderson were doomed
for frustration because they were black geniuses.
Jazz was a whore
until Duke dressed her up in a negligee of
                                   African velvet.
The Birth of the Cool
              Jeru/Budo/Venus de Milo/
              and a Saint named Miles
Jazz at the Philharmonic
              battle of tenors/Jacquet/
              Stitt and a little brown
              Jug named Ammons.

God bless Count Basie
for preserving the blues.
Evolution continues even though Coltrane

                                                    is dead.

And a new wave of jazz lovers is buried.

DUDLEY RANDALL

Langston Blues

Your lips were so laughing
Langston man
Your lips were so singing
Minstrel man
How death could touch them
Hard to understand

Your lips that laughed
And sang so well
Your lips that brought
Laughter from hell
Are silent now
No more to tell

So let us sing
A Langston blues
Sing a lost
Langston blues
Long-gone song
For Langston Hughes

EUGENE B. REDMOND

Distance

I am still on fire.

The flames in my veins and heart
Boil blood and burn hissing-hot.

Yet my time is inched on
By the realization of each new
Gleam-in-a-father's-eye.

My wrinkled oval sacks
Have pumped a sea of come
Up through a mercenary-muscle
Into vaginas, wet towels and mouths.
But each sapping of the glistening love-sauce
Creates a new supply—
Like the Phoenix Bird that rises from its own ashes.

More and more, like James Brown,
I find myself saying "I used to . . . . there was a time."

The mind grows younger and remembers:
The poetic but unprophetic words of my grandmother
        as she played
Tick-tack-toe on my butt with an ironing cord:
"You little black bastard; Nigger, you won't live to be 21
With your mannish tail";
Parking piously in the park to finger-fuck and poke pussy
        after dark;
Coming three times-in-a-row;
Crawling through wives' windows;
Whole weeks of whiskey and whaling without sleep;
Palating pills, inhaling hashish, sucking syrup,
And gurgling O'Grady in a 1-2-3-4-fashion.

The items mount memory's totempole:
The wild gossip of *Lady Day;*
The trips of *Yard Bird;*
The passion and elegance of *Mr. B;*
The legacy of *Chano Pozo;*
The hum of *Midnighters,*
Drifters,
Coasters
And *Orioles;*
The mood, mind and myths of *Miles.*

A single life,
A daily diet of death and
Under the bludgeoning of the slave drivers call
I am bound and thrown
At the feet of a white Christ

157

Where vultures stab and snap with putrid beaks at my
    eye balls.

I now know distance and dread:
        rivers and voices
        freedom in a cage
        freedom in a cage
Distance calls. In my secret soul heroes have always been
    black.
But America raised me on
John Wayne
Shirley Temple
And Tarzan.

America gave me distance!
America gave me distance!

Now, while I am still on fire,
I ache in anger to get home.

DAVID RIVARD

Baby Vallejo

Take the night Myron Stout shut his sure blind eyes,
his pale head tilted awhile, smiling
and swaying to an Eric Dolphy solo, or that morning
a sea otter, having fed, preened in the cove
below Tomales Bay, wolf-gray & magpie-black—
both times
it was easy to feel how each
left his mark on me. Out of my happiness
they carved an intensity. Though the same could be said
of my hatred. Take the moment
my grip loosened so I couldn't stop my cousin
from punching out his wife. His mark shaped
like a stony, contemptible hand,
but even its
lines flawlessly chiseled,
cunning, still coaxing me, even now, to go inside myself
to look it over. No matter who made them
I love each of these marks, whoever it was
whispering or shouting near me. Nostalgia

has nothing to do with it, & neither loneliness nor grief.
Again & again I go
into myself to study them, bypassing only
that mark fashioned
in June of 1976, set there by a worried face, a phlegmy voice
which asked me why a bus should swerve into a crowded plaza,
a school bus, blue, gutted of seats,
soldier at the wheel. Why the washed-out
white insignia stencilled
on its hood? Inside, men hang by their wrists,
naked, beside
two dead calves, two flayed & stiffened
carcasses swinging on meat hooks
as the bus pulls over.
                              It was simply a dream,
and the man recounting it, a Pakistani tile mason, wanted only
the least implausible interpretation. But I never answered,
out of ignorance or indifference,
some job site superstition. I stood with him, silent,
at that development where I slapped up
dry wall for a two-bit Boston contractor.
Hands grizzled by dried grouting pastes,
he spoke the concise, elaborated English a former lecturer
in linguistics might—
since, in fact, that is what he had once been,
that & a cipher for the wrong politics—his words filtered
through a crushed windpipe, a nose
smashed during several precisely-engineered, & official, beatings
in Karachi. Suffice it to say
the mark carved inside me
by that voice is probably exquisite, intricate,
as grave & sinuous as the greying hairs
of the beard that covered his scars.
But I don't go in to look
it over. Because he knows why
in my poems a querulous gray rain sometimes sweeps down,
and, knowing, refuses
to believe, as I do, that the roofs of our houses,
of the huts & pavilions & civic centers,
will withstand the rain's buffeting,
why, in other words,
sadly, happily, luxuriously, it is often
Rivard against Rivard.

CONRAD KENT RIVERS

Underground

(black cat)

Under bright city lights
I swing on rusty water pipes
like a wolf running wacky
across high circus wires.

I frequent basement parlors
where jazz freaks a blonde
drunk on black jazzmen blowing
sartonian melodies.

In air-cooled clean apartments where
dim darkness is defined powerless
by a parted sun patently and
niggardly going berserk, baby,
in the first person singular
I swing through the city full of blues.

JEREMY ROBSON

Blues for the Lonely*

Now the birds begin to crow.   It is time for them to crow.
Below, hurrying cars have almost reached their destinations
The crowded trains shrug slowly from the stations.
Soon they will be gone   Only gaping stars lonely
and unwatched guard the sleeping city   The branches chatter
in the breeze   the grass softens under the falling dew.

For some there is sleep,   for others only pitiless joltings
from uncertain memories,   For some sleep comes in an
overwhelming cloud,   hurrying them past smiling suns
to a Never-Never-land of warmth and kindness.

But for most night brings a cover with cruel transparencies
So for me.   It is as if a blind man felt suddenly for his stick,

and there were no stick   or called softly for his dog,
and there were no dog.   There is no shelter, no cloak
to hide behind,   only question marks enquiring from the sky.

Seeing her spread contentedly on the sheets,   you know for
the first time that you are strangers and you know everyone
is a stranger.   Desire changes to demand   You want
to run but there's no-where to run to   You want to
shout but there's no-one to listen.   So you
pretend and smile shake-hands and drink and smoke
and yell love in everybody's face.   And they tell you
you're a hell of a guy   and you believe them.

You believe them until you're alone   until you lie staring at
the silence and the hundred questions illuminated in the sky.

★Written to the track "Blue in Green" of the Miles Davis record *Kind of Blue*.

CAROLYN M. RODGERS

We Dance Like Ella Riffs

the room was a
red glow, there was
a warm close pulsating.
Chairs and tables were
                    sprawled like a semi-circle
bowing to the band stand where
                        ripples of light lingered
on the silver tracings of player's
soulpieces and
brightened and glistened and
dazzjangled
like tear drops
in a corner
            suspended
and spit on by the light
                    again and again and oooooh

161

Written for Love of an Ascension—Coltrane

he tried to
climb a
ladder of light
veiled in mist/incessantly
vacillating

tried to
trap that
wheezy harmony that
solders quarters notes
on to our heads and

melts down minds like
molten lead, ejaculates
rhythm, curses prayers, then
rings our ends like
shattering crystals

till a melody orgasm
explodes in our heads—
it's the sax, a feeling
geyser splattering the
sky

gushing and spblaring
to relieve itself with
notes that stalk and
split the clouds or that
rip the air into rifts of

whines for a jagged crescendo, a man
a velvet willow suspended in air

with his roots
stretching to plant
themselves
                    in
                          any
star.

Bunk Johnson Blowing

*in memory of Leadbelly
and his house on 59th Street*

They found him in the fields and called him back to music.
Can't, he said, my teeth are gone.   They bought him teeth.

Bunk Johnson's trumpet on a California
early May evening, calling me to
breath of . . .
up those stairs . . .
calling me to
look into
the face of that
trumpet
experience
and past it
his eyes

Jim and Rita beside me. We drank it. Jim had just come back
from Sacramento the houses made of piano boxes the bar
    without
a sign and the Mexicans drinking we drank the trumpet music
and drank that black park moonlit beneath the willow trees,
Bunk Johnson blowing all night out of that full moon.
Two-towered church. Rita listening to it, all night
music! said, I'm supposed to, despise them.
Tears streaming down her face. Said, don't tell my ancestors.

We three slid down that San Francisco hill.

Homage to Literature

When you imagine trumpet-faced musicians
blowing again inimitable jazz
no art can accuse nor cannonadings hurt,

or coming out of your dreams of dirigibles
again see the unreasonable cripple
throwing his crutch headlong as the headlights

163

streak down the torn street, as the three hammerers
go One, Two, Three on the stake, triphammer poundings
and not a sign of new worlds to still the heart;

then stare into the lake of sunset as it runs
boiling, over the west past all control

rolling and swamps the heartbeat and repeats
sea beyond sea after unbearable suns;
think: poems fixed this landscape: Blake, Donne, Keats.

SADIQ

Tuskegee Experiment

1. while Sidney Bechet was
    pullin' pistols in Paris,
    Nurse Rivers, who even
    had a car to shuffle her
    syphilitic children across
    Macon County, her "bad
    blood" cotton pickers,
    the "joy" of her life,
    was clearly chosen.
    an appointment befitting
    this darkest century.

2. a Dr. Clark conviction
    a Dr. Wenger coversion
    a Dr. Vonderlehr conception
    a Dr. Peters spinal puncture
    a Dr. Dibble hanging from
    his ankles in the town square,
    the Surgeon General's *schwartzegeist* rising,
    while Tuskegee falls asleep.

3. bring them to autopsy
    with ulcerated limbs,
    with howling wives,
    bring them in, one coon corpse at a time.
    (says Dr. Dibble,)
    "a dollar a year for forty years

to watch these shadows rot."
"they didn't receive treatment for syphilis,
but they got so much else.
medicine is as much art as it is science."

4. a row of crows on a rickety fence.
   no book learnin'.
   po' as dirt,
   never heard Monsieur Bechet
   play the clarinet.
   this experiment is not a crime,
   but a rite of sacrifice

5. no banana splits on sunday,
   no Brooks Brothers,
   no color t.v. & waterbed,
   no tickets to the county fair.
   no treatment! no treatment!
   no treatment! no treatment!

NTOZAKE SHANGE

Elegance in the Extreme

for Cecil Taylor

elegance in the extreme
gives style to the hours
of coaxing warmth outta
no where

elegant hoodlums
elegant intellectuals
elegant ornithologists
elegant botanists

but elegance in the extreme helps most
the stranger who hesitates
to give what there is
for fear of unleashing madness
which is sometimes

uninvolved in contemporary mores
archetypal realities or graciousness

in the absence of extreme elegance
madness can set right in like
a burnin gauloise on japanese silk
though highly cultured
even the silk must ask
how to burn up discreetly

CHARLES SIMIC

Crepuscule with Nellie

for Ira

Monk at the Five Spot
    late one night.
Ruby my Dear, Epistrophy.
    The place nearly empty
Because of the cold spell.
One beautiful black transvestite
    alone up front,
Sipping his drink demurely.

The music Pythagorean,
    one note at a time
Connecting the heavenly spheres,
While I leaned against the bar
    surveying the premises
Through cigarette smoke.

All of a sudden, a clear sense
    of a memorable occasion . . .
The joy of it, the delicious melancholy . . .
This very strange man bent over the piano
    shaking his head, humming . . .

Misterioso.

Then it was all over, thank you!
Chairs being stacked up on tables,
    their legs up.

The prospect of the freeze outside,
	the long walk home,
Making one procrastinatory.

Who said Americans don't have history,
	only endless nostalgia?
And where the hell was Nellie?

RALPH SNEEDEN

Coltrane and My Father

Late one night I hear his breath
between runs, something the mikes
couldn't hide, what vinyl
makes us forget: the man
behind the instrument. My father
had seen him once, said that on a solo
he went too far out and never came back.
People started leaving.

Across the room the tiny lights
of the tape deck blink in sympathy
with the horn's voice but register
nothing when he pauses to inhale, or sigh
with sudden joy, fatigue, disbelief.

A home movie: the barren, snowless slope
at Squaw Valley, summer, 1961;
my mother grows smaller
as a swinging chairlift carries her
and the infant in her arms
slowly into invisibility, and for a moment,
a stream of blue cigarette smoke
glides in front of the camera
from nowhere,
then out of sight to the left.

A. B. SPELLMAN

Did John's Music Kill Him?

in the morning part
of evening he would stand
before his crowd. the voice
would call his name &
redlight fell around him.
jimmy'd bow a quarter hour
till Mccoy fed block chords
to his stroke. elvin's thunder
roll & eric's scream. then john.

then john. *little old lady*
had a nasty mouth. *summertime*
when the war is. *africa* ululating
a line bunched up like itself
into knots paints beauty black.

trane's horn had words in it
i know when i sleep sober & dream
those dreams i duck in the world
of sun & shadow. yet even in the day john
& a little grass put them on me clear
as tomorrow in a glass enclosure.

kill me john my life eats
life. the thing that beats out of
me happens in a vat enclosed
& fermenting & wanting to explode
like your song.

> so beat john's death words down
> on me in the darker part
> of evening. the black light issued
> from him in the pit he made
> around us. worms came clear
> to me where i thought i had been
> brilliant. o john death will
> not contain you death
> will not contain you

John Coltrane

an impartial review.

may he have new life like the fall
fallen tree, wet moist rotten enough
to see shoots stalks branches & green
leaves (& may the roots) grow into his side.

around the back of the mind, in its closet
is a string, i think, a coil around things.
listen to *summertime*, think of spring, negroes
cats in the closet, anything that makes a rock

of your eye. imagine you steal. you are frightened
you want help. you are sorry you are born with ears.

LORENZO THOMAS

Historiography

Bird is a god of good graciousness.
   —Ted Joans

1

The junkies loved Charles Parker and the sports
And the high living down looking ones
Those who loved music and terror and lames
Who in Bird's end would someday do better

As the Bird spiralled down in disaster
Before the TV set some would come to prefer
Out of the sadness of Mr Parker's absence
Never again hearing the strings of Longines

Symphonette

Without hearing the keening cry of the Bird
Nailed to the wax they adored. In the memories
And warmth of their bodies where our Bird
Stays chilly and gone. Every cat caught with

A white girl wailed Bird Lives! And the dopies
Who loved Charlie Parker made his memory live
Those who loved music made his memory live
And made the young ones never forget Bird

Was a junkie

2

We lost others to pain stardom and
Some starved at vicious banquets
Where they played until the victuals
Was gone. Pretty music. For all that

Pain. Who made the young ones remember the pain
And almost forget the dances? Who did that?
Steal the prints and the master and burn down
The hope of his rage when he raged? It was

Not only pain

There was beauty and longing. And Love run
Down like the cooling waters from heaven
And sweat off the shining black brow. Bird
Was thinking and singing. His only thought

Was a song. He saw the truth. And shout the Truth
Where Indiana was more than the dim streets of Gary
A hothouse of allegedly fruitful plain America
Some will never forgive the brother for that. Bird

Was a junkie

3

According to my records, there was something
More. There was space. Seeking. And mind
Bringing African control on the corny times
Of the tunes he would play. There was Space

And the Sun and the Stars he saw in his head
In the sky on the street and the ceilings
Of nightclubs and Lounges as we sought to
Actually lounge trapped in the dull asylum

Of our own enslavements. But Bird *was* a junkie!

170

ASKIA MUHAMMAD TOURÉ

JuJu

for John Coltrane, Priest-prophet
of the Black Nation

The Opening
(From the Chronicle)

" . . . and They were there in the City of Fire, enflamed
Their souls burnin' and a'thirstin' for the Light—
the Rain, the Water of the Soul, extinguished by
the Long Whiplash of the Dead.
And They cried out to God to deliver them, or send
a bit of Light from Eternity to let Them know that
He really cared, still cared.
So He sent Geniuses, Magic Men of Old:
Scientists and Prophets, Scholars and Sages,
Philosophers and Myth-making Priests.
Garvey and DuBois, Langston and Booker T.,
Bessie and Satchmo, Bird and Lady Day,
Malcolm and Elijah, Otis and Aretha—
and John Coltrane.
And this Last, this is his Testament, his Requiem, his
dues-payin' Eulogy: John Coltrane . . ."

The Pain

Tone. Blue skies and flowing fountains.
Flowering spring-trees, trees, away from here now,
this blooming inwardly as the Soul flows and grows
to newer vistas higher than before.
This journey to the Source of love, garden in the core
of life, tone, this ever-aching loneliness or need
to meet the matchless rhythms of the heart.

Take him now heart and soul of Life—essence wonder
blowing wind of love-change and sounds of Blackness
born of Mother Earth.
Tone. Brown and ebon hue shackled with the matchless

171

chains of Time. Born blood born tone of dripping
screaming sheets of sound, born bleeding with the
dripping wound of Lash and shrieking mindless pain
grown silent with the flow of silent years.

Down trash-blown streets among the tragic mass of shrunken
twisted shells of warriors wine-soaked, dope-bent Blackmen
once proud seed of pulsing loins thrilling to
the touch of Summer rain.

Take him! Take him! to your wombs, to your bosoms
Mothers, Harlem! Africa!—
strong and vibrant with your love.
He Priest Prophet Warrior call and Clarion Call
of essence—US, BLACKNESS—as in Eastern swan-tone
cry of pale towers falling, burning in the bitter
Fires of Change.

Or Eric in Paris, pain growing madly from his genius heart
like strange flowers of our ever-present death.
Death here, death there; they go from us, all giants:
MALCOLM! ERIC! OTIS! LANGSTON!—
now the Prophet Warrior Priest of Blackness: TRANE!
go TRANE go TRANE away in essence of blue-sky tone
hunger Black loneliness of nightdeath calling
through Eastern regions of the Heart:
TRANE! TRANE! TRANE!

The Joy

Down vistas of light I hear him call me, my
brother magic piper of
Visions of Now.
His horn cascading fountains of blood and bones and stormy
rainbows firedarts purple blue-song tear-stained
channels of love.
Past green beast-eyes and the carnal leer of lust and hate
we wander sad in our soul-song, big as life and warm
as throbbing Earth loamy in the crystal rain of Spring.

We, poet and magic myth-making Giant of Song, wander on.
Holy the bones of our ancestors wrapped in Pyramids
    resting till the end of Time.

Holy the Magi, priests and Myth-scientists of Africa
        for sending him to us.
He with Eternity upon his horn cascading diamonds of Destiny
to our blues-ridden hearts crushed against the Towers
        of the West.
O Magic! to live dynamic in the Soul against the deadly
concrete and steel blaring trumpets—Hell gazing from
        the blue killer-eyes.

Solo   Solo   Solo   for Africanic joys: rhythm thrilling from
the mobile hips of choclit mamas Bird-of-Paradise pagan colors
Joy vibrating from the rat-nests of the West.
And greens and cornbread, sweet potatoes boogalooing
        in the brilliance of his smile.

PRAISE BE TO:
                Africa, Mother of the Sphinx,
who brought our souls back from the Land
                        of the Dead.

PRAISE BE TO:
                the Old Ones:
Magi in pyramidal silence who
made the JuJu in our blood outlast
the Frankenstein of the West.

PRAISE BE TO:
                Thutmose and Hermes
    Piankhi and Nefertari
                Songhai
        and Dahomey—
                    Ghana and Benin

laugh with purple gums, nigger lips, shiny teeth
at the resurrection of their seed amid
gunfire in the Harlems of the West.

PRAISE BE TO:
        ALLAH
who brought us Malcolm and Elijah
and reopened Islam like a Flaming Torch
to elevate our souls and send us
soaring to the mountains of the Black World
seeking Paradise.

And through it all the echoes of his horn
blowing Joy thrilling golden fountains Love and Beauty
flowing Spring and dark witch-eyes, full nigger-lips,
wooly hair like Dionne/'Retha singing us to Blackness
sprouting from our genes sprouting in the wine-flush
of our blood to course into our full-expanding Minds
and lift us high upon a hill above the ghetto death-traps
past Suffering and Want past Heartbreak and Heartache to
        Eternity and God—and he is
NOT gone for I can see, can hear him still: my Heart
        my Soul my All vibrating—TRANE!

> *"A LOVE   SUPREME*
> *A LOVE   SUPREME*
> *A LOVE   SUPREME*
> *A LOVE   SUPREME*
> *A LOVE   SUPREME*
> *A LOVE   SUPREME*
> *A LOVE   SUPREME . . . ."*

O Lord of Light! A Mystic Sage Returns to Realms of Eternity!

for Master Sun Ra/ Sonny Blount
(May 22, 1914–May 30, 1993)

I

He is sun-bright myth and Cosmic Light,
the audaciousness of comets sweeping through the inky abyss
        of night,
the Solar Lord as pharaoh of magic, mega-sounds, harmonious
with spectacular delights and unbridled flights aboard
        the Melanin rocketship bound for the funk planets.
Ja man of Jupiterian wisdom, crowned prince of immortal night:
        Lord Sun-Ra renamed,
renowned, resplendent in sparkling, sequined satins;
solar disc ablaze like a living Uraeus, working his aural magic
among the tropic myths of reborn Kamites. In the kingdoms
of his liberated soul, in realms of resurgent Negritude, we
        celebrate his audacity, his expanded vision of

174

Possibility; moving beyond plastic parameters
of Anglo blandness, into multidimensional
space-time continuums,
restoring the broad-ranged, epic Consciousness of Cosmic Music,
embodied in a galaxy of master compositions, Alchemical
solos featuring Coltrane and Pharoah,
Don and Albert Ayler, Ornette Coleman, Sunny Murray, Milford Graves,
Marion Brown and myriad masters embracing
sacred pillars of the Sky Lords, Immortal Mansions of Ra.

II

He has moved beyond us, riding Shango's lightning into stellar
parameters; a Moon Lord, changing his coat
arrayed in cosmic colors; hanging with Tehuti, embracing azure robes
of Isis, soloing with Bird Diz Miles among expanses of inter-galactic
space ways, riding bursts of super-novas
brighter than a million mushroom bombs. A living Ancestor now
with Larry Neal, Henry Dumas
legendary visionaries embodying all of our
sterling strengths, imaginative flights, volcanic passion, spanning
generations of Captivity and Resistance, deep pain
wild joy—the Cosmic Lord resplendent among us;
solar obelisk of myth, long-breath solo of God-voice surging in
symphonies of light, phoenix flight of bright Bennu, delighting
myriad choruses of angels, Orishas, who
dance upon sun beams of his extended solos: O Lord of Light,
O Sun Prince transporting our tropic memories to emerald
mountains rising above primordial jungle dawns;
O Sky Lord roaring a Horus mantra in a dark abyss of Caucasian-
Neanderthal hell;
O Father, Osirian mage waving your pharaonic baton above choruses of
saxophones, posses of trumpets, bevies of thundering Afrikan drums
shaking the earth like Zulu legions.

III

We mourn you when Whirlwinds roar and embrace our Marcus Garvey
rhapsodies above Middle Passage moans;
We mourn you when Midnight glides into our Consciousness wearing
a white gardenia above her
Billie Holiday face; when Sassy Vaughan launches her indigo-velvet
voice upon the mantras of our ecstasies.

We sing you, Father Ra-Osiris, asking that our memories continue
in your voyages to farthest reaches of the Universe, that they
form a ring around your Solar Disc as
monumental love vibrations; for you are our heart, our elder sage
and parent, our cosmological thrust into parameters of Infinity,
an epiphany of Cosmic compassion
mounting summits of Divinity, an archetypal surge of Harmony
within temples of Maatic Eternity;
in Pyramids and mythic shadows, in sunbursts and meteor showers,
in Whirlwinds riding glowing episodes of ritual Nirvana; O Sage,
we wish you long life in transcendental vistas
amid pristine solos raising the Dead;
We ask that Ra, mounting
His Barque of Millions of Years, welcome His son
into infinite realms of joy, Mansions
of the Cosmic Light!

DEREK WALCOTT

Blues

Those five or six young guys
hunched on the stoop
that oven-hot summer night
whistled me over. Nice
and friendly. So, I stop.
MacDougal or Christopher
Street in chains of light.

A summer festival. Or some
saint's. I wasn't too far from
home, but not too bright
for a nigger, and not too dark.
I figured we were all
one, wop, nigger, jew,
besides, this wasn't Central Park.
I'm coming on too strong? You figure
right! They beat this yellow nigger
black and blue.

Yeah. During all this, scared
in case one used a knife,
I hung my olive-green, just-bought
sports coat on a fire plug.
I did nothing. They fought
each other, really. Life
gives them a few kicks,
that's all. The spades, the spicks.

My face smashed in, my bloody mug
pouring, my olive-branch jacket saved
from cuts and tears,
I crawled four flights upstairs.
Sprawled in the gutter, I
remember a few watchers waved
loudly, and one kid's mother shouting
like "Jackie" or "Terry,"
"now that's enough!"
It's nothing really.
They don't get enough love.

You know they wouldn't kill
you. Just playing rough,
like young America will.
Still, it taught me something
about love. If it's so tough,
forget it.

The Glory Trumpeter

Old Eddie's face, wrinkled with river lights,
Looked like a Mississippi man's. The eyes,
Derisive and avuncular at once,
Swivelling, fixed me. They'd seen
Too many wakes, too many cathouse nights.
The bony, idle fingers on the valves
Of his knee-cradled horn could tear
Through "Georgia on My Mind" or "Jesus Saves"
With the same fury of indifference
If what propelled such frenzy was despair.

Now, as the eyes sealed in the ashen flesh,
And Eddie, like a deacon at his prayer,
Rose, tilting the bright horn, I saw a flash
Of gulls and pigeons from the dunes of coal
Near my grandmother's barracks on the wharves,
I saw the sallow faces of those men
Who sighed as if they spoke into their graves
About the Negro in America. That was when
The Sunday comics, sprawled out on her floor,
Sent from the States, had a particular odour;
Dry smell of money mingled with man's sweat.

And yet, if Eddie's features held our fate,
Secure in childhood I did not know then
A jesus-ragtime or gut-bucket blues
To the bowed heads of lean, compliant men
Back from the States in their funereal serge,
Black, rusty homburgs and limp waiters' ties,
Slow, honey accents and lard-coloured eyes,
Was Joshua's ram's horn wailing for the Jews
Of patient bitterness or bitter siege.

Now it was that, as Eddie turned his back
On our young crowd out fêting, swilling liquor,
And blew, eyes closed, one foot up, out to sea,
His horn aimed at those cities of the Gulf,
Mobile and Galveston, and sweetly meted
Their horn of plenty through his bitter cup,
In lonely exaltation blaming me
For all whom race and exile have defeated,
For my own uncle in America,
That living there I never could look up.

BARRY WALLENSTEIN

Blues 1

You
catch my breath with your waking

a calf moves closer to its mother
(slumbering)

some brother leaves his home
to bring me what I need.
It doesn't work & I call you back—

Sugar—I call you Sugar

no rest in my slumber
no sugar in my bowl.

Blues 2

Such accidents do happen
dancing: she says
I'm dancing beneath your loving blow
so I stagger

staggered, he says no:
it wasn't a blow
it was a brush—feather light;
I fly round the world for your gold

another time
she tries so hard
to make him well,
it makes her sleepy

more lately
they share their tricks
but never their secrets
set in codes, dark and changing.
They can barely read what they say,
and when they do, they forget.

BELLE WARING

Refuge at the One Step Down

Shrapnel lives in Morton's neck, so his head stays
cocked to the left. We've changed generations,
man. Our waitress, sporting seven different
earrings, was born the year Morton pitched
his Purple Heart over the White House fence & then

split for Cuba & then came home to report: Nixon's
an asshole, Fidel's an asshole. It does
further one to have somewhere to go.
                                    When Morton
OD'd and got the tubes slapped down him without
one single splendid vision of his own white light,
sure, I went to see him. We used to sneak into
the One Step Down, underage, where Monk's still on
the jukebox. Then I busted out on a scholarship.
Morton went to Nam.
                        Right now Monk's playing "Misterioso"
and Morton's feeding me coffee and his arms
smooth and clean as a puppy's underbelly
making me laugh. Wide awake for swing
shift at the halfway house, he leans across the table
and says real soft, "I could teach you to meditate." Me
I want to be unconscious. Morton says, "That ain't
quite right."
                The fog is rolled up into my head. Sunday
night always gets me depressed—dragging down Columbia Road
the winos holler Lady! Talk, Lady! in Spanish & English
the pigeons hover in the torched-out windows and then

I hear my name and HEY GIRL—big hug. Let's say
you give up and ride the bus eighteen hours sore and sad.
This time nobody's talking. Morton is the moment
you open the door after a long ride home in the dark.

WEATHERLY

Mud Water Shango

a big muddy daddy my daddys gris-gris to the world.
i'm a big muddy daddy daddys gris-gris to the world.
got a mojo chop for sweet black belt girl.

daddys a river & my mamas shore is black.
daddys a river mamas shore is black.
flood coming mama you cant keep it back.

lightning in my eyes mama thunder in your soul.
theres lightning in my eyes mama thunder in your soul.
i'm a river hip daddy mama dig a muddy hole.

180

Times

truly alone muley
knows truce death music
never muted heart
knows moody brute hurts
human blows sound blues.

RON WELBURN

Ben Webster: "Did You Call Her Today?"

we do not care if you were
gruff and robust in
your ways. your music was

more than enough. she might
not care about the careless
love pumping through your powerful tenor.

did you call her? she
waited, vacillating between the
sofa's magazines and

the refrigerator; might have
visited the neighbors upstairs
or gone for your scotch or gin,

but she wasn't gone long
for you, even left the phone
off the hook. wasn't

with sweets, man, sweets
was with you, remember? asking
if you'd call her today.

hours we fight living are
often shy. if we don't know who
you are, on the street,

the ogre staring out
from froggy eyes at us.
some get you to

do a rockhinge scene
but while you were there
did you ever make that call?

do a ladyland scene
but did you speak
to her today?

sure glad
I heard about that affair
in my youth.

Bones and Drums

for Lewis McMillan

Generations unfold from our faces.
You will find kwanza celebrants
and bearers of yoruba, ibo, and muslim
names with connections in the cherokee,
gestures among the chickasaw;
a hoop broken like the faces, mouths,
a few brows native to apalachicola,
catawba, creek and the ramapos.

Has America ever noticed
how some of these voices match
the trombone? the big horn of
Big Chief Russell Moore,
Big Green, Snub Mosley,
the Jack Teagarden we speak of;
does America recall Shunatona
at the '28 Inaugural?
What does it know of Willie Colon,
Steve Turre and so many salseros
in this bull eagle's timbre of speaking.

Have they listened to the bass,
a tree of rhythm smooth as Blanton,
sinewy as Pettiford, thickset as Mingus,
supple as a Rozie.

Or drums, Baby Lovett to Sunny Murray,
for a basic two-step
a round dance grass dance beat
on the stretched snare hide of ponca city,
tishomingo, okmulgee, tahlequa,
the rolling piano of muskogee;
sock cymbals and high hats
of seed beads, patterned and flowing
like leaves in a river
in the split accents of 4/4.

Gonsalves

crescendoes are indigo scarves
women wear in the new england autumns
diminuendoes the sky overcast
by whisky and evil moods.
rhode island is a whisker
on the chin of obatala
and festivals are light years
in the memory. exiled,
the mood of a song comes into the bay,
a *mornas* all the way from
cabo verde, a place not far
from guinea.

MILLER WILLIAMS

The Death of Chet Baker

Somewhere between *Amazing Grace*
and *Great Balls of Fire* we heard
the horn first and then the voice
like Billie Holiday's. Old Bird,

he knew a secret. So did Diz.
But Chet, he struck him up a deal
with dark angels. Angel he was
and dark he was. Truth to tell,

he darkened till he fell away
wearing twice his fitting years,
still playing at what he had to say,
sometimes putting on some airs

but they were his. He put them on
like pants and shoes, a wrinkled shirt.
What do we feel, now that he's gone?
What of the hollow? How does it hurt?

Hotly as shame? Sharply as scorn?
As dimly as an old rebuke?
There was a hophead with a horn
who stopped a concert to puke,

who couldn't read the notes he played,
who couldn't love a person long,
who blew the breath of souls afraid
into muted, seamless song.

But what to pity these pitiless days?
He had his dreams and methadone,
we have tapes and CDs,
Time after Time, When Your Lover Has Gone.

CDs do what was done before
over and over and over and over,
never adding a note more
if we should listen to them forever.

Wherever we are he isn't there.
Love him. Love him in the loss
for all the things he did with air.
The Thrill Is Gone. Poor Chet. Poor us.

Epitaph
Once a Jazzman, playing high,
raised up his horn and tried to fly.
He got above the oxygen
and fell back to earth again.
The body here beneath this stone
was Chet Baker, who has flown.

DAVID WOJAHN

John Berryman Listening to Robert Johnson's "King of the Delta Blues," January 1972

Am I a dead man? Am I a dead man?
—Hards to say, Mr. Bones, could be.
I think some hellhound's got the scent of me.
Hear him, I do, often.
He stands like Henry's father in the black room
Filled with light. Henry's childhood home.

And Henry, like him, is undone,
Conjuring him, conjuring him.
Mad Robert Johnson did traffic with ghosts,
Which hurt themselves, coming to their lifes again.
—Why, now, Sir Bones, you messin' wif' dem?
Henry's terrible lost,

Though Henry has lived, longer by much
Than Robert Johnson, who met the devil at a crossroads,
Dead at 26.
Hellhound, truly, *do* exist.
And Henry will not sing more, either. He loads
The gin with ice cube, lemon twist.

BARON WORMSER

It's a Party (1959)

The rhododendron is happy. Its aloof yet sexual
    blossoms glimmer in the cool April moonlight.
The pebbles in the driveway croon very softly.
The Negro ceramic jockey, which towards the end of the next
    decade the children who are now asleep in
    their Snuggy-Pooh pajamas will unceremoniously
    smash as a honky, racist artifact, extends an arm
    of welcome.

185

People drink, eat and talk elaborately:
>   It's the death of Charlie Parker
>   A grandma who swims laps at the Y each day
>   Crabcakes
>   Zoning bribes
>   Sartre's existential pride.
If everyone is aware of everyone else,
>   everyone is unconcerned too.
The halftones of sex
>   craft a jauntily steamy mood
>   of nods and titters, long and longer looks.
It's
Eric Dolphy
Trane
Charles Mingus
No one is peeved or grumpy,
>   no one complains how life wronged him or her,
>   no one bitches about how this was not
>   the planet he or she ordered.
It's
Life in the big adrenaline city
Life in shackroof, deputy sheriff Mississippi
Life in a Nash Rambler, looking out
>   windows at oblivious trees.

Winks and shrugs as soft as rayon.
People muse and kiss.

Someone in black pants is lying on his back.
Someone is thumbing through a book from the big bookcase.
Someone is downing other people's drinks:
>   bourbon, Scotch, sloe gin.
There's nothing like reading Proust when you're drunk.
There's nothing like touching someone's skin
>   you've wanted to touch for hours.
There's nothing like delivering an enlightened opinion
>   and laughing at yourself seconds later
>   for being so stiflingly correct.

Someone hoots like a wellbred owl.
Someone flings peanuts into his mouth.

Someone yawns fiercely
    as the jazz, the lofty gritty searching
    elegantly churning jazz
    the sympathetic overheard genius plays on.

JAY WRIGHT

The End of an Ethnic Dream

Cigarettes in my mouth
to puncture blisters in my brain.
My bass a fine piece of furniture.
My fingers soft, too soft to rattle
rafters in second-rate halls.
The harmonies I could never learn
stick in Ayler's screams.
An African chant chokes us. My image shot.

If you look off over the Hudson,
the dark cooperatives spit at the dinghies
floating up the night.

    A young boy pisses
on lovers rolling against each other
under a trackless el.

  This could have been my town,
with light strings that could stand a tempo.

    Now,
    it's the end
    of an ethnic dream.

I've grown intellectual,
go on accumulating furniture and books,
damning literature, writing "for myself,"
calculating the possibilities that someone
will love me, or sleep with me.
Eighteen-year-old girls come back from the Southern
leers and make me cry.

    Here, there are
    coffee shops, bars,

natural tonsorial parlors,
plays, streets,
pamphlets, days, sun,
heat, love, anger,
politics, days, and sun.

Here, we shoot off
every day to new horizons,
coffee shops, bars,
natural tonsorial parlors,
plays, streets,
pamphlets, days, sun,
heat, love, anger,
politics, days, and sun.

It is the end of an ethnic dream.
My bass is a fine piece of furniture.
My brain blistered.

YEVGENY YEVTUSHENKO

Saints of Jazz

(translated by Albert C. Todd)

The Saints of Jazz are playing.
Gray hair shakes to the beat,
and oldness, of course, is terrible,
but like youth, it comes just once.

Senile quick movement is sad,
yet age is younger than youth,
when a youngster grown wiser
pounds the keys within.

Looking like a kitchen cook,
the mulattress cross-handed
bangs jauntily on a baby grand,
and, fat and black, it dances away.

Without envy for green youngsters,
an old codger clowns on a trumpet,

and his unbuttoned collar
plunges into a mug of beer.

His neighbor lists decrepitly,
but with a cagey wanton in his eyes,
he plucks the double bass
like a gorgeous giggling girl.

The drummer's hands are a ballet.
Where's old age in a gray-haired tomboy?
Like a white lady, a smile
dances on the black face.

Their throats and thoughts are hoarse,
but the sounds are refreshing and youthful—
now slack, like the Mississippi,
now, like Niagara, stormy and wild.

Ah, how much the jazz artists
of all countries have stolen from here,
but nevertheless New Orleans
was not taken from New Orleans.

The Saints of Jazz are playing—
magnificent old people.
You, our blasphemer-age, be compassionate—
safeguard at least these Saints!

Earth's not crowded with saints,
and if it's up to us,
then let there be art—
jazz, at least, as last resort.

The harsh slave market of the stage
wrings dry its slaves,
and if the slaves are a trifle old,
they will be hidden in a grand piano of graves.

Life goes skidding downhill,
and if there is no way out,
then to the blues let it roll on,
ringing twilight in the end.

Sunset is not the end for a poet,
nor is death for you, musician.
The eternal strength of dawn
is in you, O noblest sunset.

Satchmo

(translated by Albert C. Todd)

Great Satchmo plays all bathed in sweat.
A salty Niagara pours from his brow,
but when the trumpet rises to the clouds,
it growls,
        it roars.
He played to the whole world
                the way he loved.
He is stolen from us now by the grave,
but even before his birth
he was stolen
        from his sweet Africa.
In secret revenge for the chains of his ancestors
he enslaves us all
        like helpless babes.
The whites of his great eyes flicker in sorrow
as he howls and horns about the globe—
this kid from an orphanage
in the town of New Orleans.
Great Satchmo plays all bathed in sweat,
his nostrils smoke
           like two black muzzles,
and teeth dazzle in his mouth
like thirty white projectors.
And the sparkling sweat pours off
as if a beautiful mighty hippo
has risen
      snorting,
          from an African river.
Stamping on fan notes with his heel,
and wiping the downpour from his brow,
he throws handkerchief after handkerchief
into the piano's open womb.
Again back to the microphone he goes,
pressing the stage till it cracks,
and each wet handkerchief is as heavy
as the crown of art.
Art is very far
from the lady whose name is Pose,

and when it labors
it's not ashamed of sweat.
Art is
          not the charm of prattlers,
but, full of movement of heavy things,
the tragic labor of a trumpet player
whose music is tatters of lung.
Though art is bartered and sold,
that's not what it's all about.
The poet
          and the great jazzman
are like brothers
                    in their rasping delivery.
Great Satchmo, will you make it to heaven?
Who knows!
          But if you do—play!
Let the good times roll once more!
Shake up
          that boring state of little angels.
But so there'll be no remorse in hell,
so death will cheer us sinners up,
Archangel Gabriel,
pass your horn
                    to the better player,
to Louis!

AL YOUNG

Dance of the Infidels

in memory of Bud Powell

The smooth smell of Manhattan taxis,
Parisian taxis, it doesnt matter, it's
the feeling that modern man is all youve
laid him out to be in those tinglings & rushes;
the simple touch of your ringed fingers
against a functioning piano.

191

The winds of Brooklyn
still mean a lot to me. The way certain chicks
formed themselves & their whole lives around
a few notes, an attitude more than anything.
I know about the being out of touch, bumming
nickels & dimes worth of this & that off
him & her here & there — everything but
hither & yon.

Genius does not grow on trees.

I owe
you a million love dollars & so much more than
thank-you for re-writing the touch & taste & smell
of the world for me those city years when I could
very well have fasted on into oblivion.

Ive just
been playing the record you made in Paris with Art
Blakey & Lee Morgan. The european audience
is applauding madly. I think of what Ive heard
of Buttercup's flowering on the Left Bank & days
you had no one to speak to. Wayne Shorter is
beautifying the background of sunlight with
children playing in it & shiny convertibles
& sedans parked along the block as I blow.

Grass
grows. Negroes. Women walk. The world, in case
youre losing touch again, keeps wanting the same
old thing.

You gave me some of it; beauty I sought
before I was even aware how much I needed it.

I know
this world is terrible & that one must, above all,
hold onto the heart & the hearts of others.

I love *you*

192

Lester Leaps In

Nobody but Lester let Lester leap
into a spotlight that got too hot
for him to handle, much less keep
under control like thirst in a drought.

He had his sensitive side, he had
his hat, that glamorous porkpie whose
sweatband soaked up all that bad
leftover energy.

                    How did he choose
those winning titles he'd lay on favorites
— Sweets Edison, Sir Charles, Lady Day?
Oooo and his sound! Once you savor its
flaming smooth aftertaste, what do you say?

Here lived a man so hard and softspoken
he had to be cool enough to hold his horn
at angles as sharp as he was heartbroken
in order to blow what it's like being born.

PAUL ZIMMER

But Bird

Some things you should forget,
But Bird was something to believe in.
Autumn '54, twenty, drafted,
Stationed near New York en route
To atomic tests in Nevada.
I taught myself to take
A train to Pennsylvania Station,
Walk up Seventh to 52nd Street,
Looking for music and legends.
One night I found the one
I wanted. Bird.

Five months later no one was brave
When the numbers ran out.
All equal—privates and colonels—
Down on our knees in the slits

193

As the voice counted backward
In the dark turning to light.

But "Charlie Parker" it said
On the Birdland marquee,
And I dug for the cover charge,
Sat down in the cheap seats.
He slumped in from the kitchen,
Powder blue serge and suedes.
No jive Bird, he blew crisp and clean,
Bringing each face in the crowd
Gleaming to the bell of his horn.
No fluffing, no wavering,
But soaring like on my old
Verve waxes back in Ohio.

Months later, down in the sand,
The bones in our fingers were
Suddenly x-rayed by the flash.
We moaned together in light
That entered everything,
Tried to become the earth itself
As the shock rolled toward us.

But Bird. I sat through three sets,
Missed the last train out,
Had to bunk in a roach pad,
Sleep in my uniform, almost AWOL.
But Bird was giving it all away,
One of his last great gifts,
And I was there with my
Rosy cheeks and swan neck,
Looking for something to believe in.

When the trench caved in it felt
Like death, but we clawed out,
Walked beneath the roiling, brutal cloud
To see the flattened houses,
Sheep and pigs blasted,
Ravens and rabbits blind,
Scrabbling in the grit and yucca.

But Bird. Remember Bird.
Five months later he was dead,

While I was down on my knees,
Wretched with fear in
The cinders of the desert.

Sitting with Lester Young

for Michael S. Harper

Dusk must become your light
If you want to see Lester Young.
So Zimmer sits beside him at
His window in the Alvin Hotel.
Pres is blue beyond redemption.
His tenor idle on the table,
He looks down at the street,
Drinking his gin and port.
Buildings slice the last light
From the day. If Pres could
Shuffle into a club again like
A wounded animal, he would
Blow his ultimate melancholy,
But nights belong to others now.
Zimmer can only watch Pres
In the half light of his sadness,
Old whispers slipping around,
Words into melodies,
As holy silence means the most.

Biographical Notes and Statements of Poetics

AI has written five collections of poetry, the latest being *Greed*. In addition to those works, she has published a novel titled *Blackout*.

"One day, I was trading in some cassettes at Zia Records here in Tempe, Arizona. I had been standing at the counter for awhile, when I realized I was standing in the center of a whirlwind of music. That music, that whirlwind, was John Coltrane, who I am convinced had achieved satori and was at that moment a teacher, a master even from the grave."

SAMUEL ALLEN, who has also published under the pen name Paul Vesey, has had a varied career as a poet, lawyer, teacher, and translator. His four collections of poetry are *Elfenbeinzahne*, a bilingual edition published in Heidelberg with translations and epilogue by Janheinz Jahn; *Ivory Tusks; Paul Vesey's Ledger*, brought out by Paul Breman as the last of his Heritage Series; and *Every Round and Other Poems*. He is the editor and one of the translators of *Poems from Africa*, and his own poetry has appeared in scores of anthologies. He is currently in the Boston area where he continues to write.

"Stephen Henderson has pointed out that music is one of two major influences on black poetry—his specific interest is in what he terms the 'new black poetry.' He spells out in considerable detail the ways in which that influence manifests itself. Jazz, in its improvisational genius, is known for the broad range, the catholicity of its expression. Nothing human is foreign; as Langston Hughes puts it, 'I dig all jive.' It incorporates any phase of experience from the solemn to a sassy irreverence, from the holy of Coltrane to the hip, from a lover's plea to explosive defiance. Hughes, the poet, exclaims (and Wynton Marsalis, the jazz artist, joins) 'Come with a blast of trumpets, *Jesus!*' and moves on elsewhere to conjure up the haunting insinuations of a saxophone. This catholic embrace of human experience is evident in both art forms.

"It is well known that particularly in black poetry, though not exclusively so, one finds the strong rhythmic stamp of the music, whether in the basic beat of a Lunceford or in the intricate rhythms of a Strayhorn.

"It is inevitable that one return to Hughes in addressing many aspects of this subject matter. One cannot think of another author in whom a jazz aesthetic is more evident. In his poetry especially, so richly informed by jazz, there is the capacity, as with jazz and its listener, to engage the reader. It is a quality powerfully present in the invocation of the spirit in traditional African religions, usually via the drum. It is the ability to move the participant and, in a dynamic of call and response, to cause the participant in turn to move. Léopold Senghor suggests in the African context this affective motion turns outward toward the other, becomes e-motion (from the Latin root *emovere*), as the invoked spirit descends. On this side of the Atlantic, it would be in voodoo and condomblé, etc. This quality is preeminent in black gospel but is shared by jazz, which is so greatly influenced by the former. They both have the means to 'take you there,' sometimes over your resistance. It is the transforming power of possession.

"I was struck in reading Toni Morrison's seminal monograph, *Playing in the Dark*, to come upon a spellbinding account of this experience in her quote of a passage from Marie Cardinal, the noted writer of French Algerian extraction. Let me conclude by simply setting forth the relevant lines:

> My first anxiety attack occurred during a Louis Armstrong concert. I was nineteen or twenty. Armstrong was going to improvise with his trumpet, to build a whole composition in which each note would be important and would contain within itself the essence of the whole. I was not disappointed: the atmosphere warmed up very fast. The scaffolding and flying buttresses of the jazz instruments supported Armstrong's trumpet, creating spaces which were adequate enough for it to climb higher, establish itself, and take off again. The sounds of the trumpet sometimes piled up together, fusing a new musical base, a sort of matrix which gave birth to one precise, unique note, tracing a sound whose path was almost painful, so absolutely had its equilibrium and duration become; it tore at the nerves of those who followed it.
>
> My heart began to accelerate, becoming more important than the music, shaking the bars of my rib cage, compressing my lungs so the air could no longer enter them. Gripped by panic at the idea of dying there in the middle of spasms, stomping feet and the crowd howling, I ran into the street like someone possessed."

BARON JAMES ASHANTI is the author of *Nubiana, Volume 1* and *Nova*, which was entered for the Pulitzer Prize for Poetry in 1991. His work has been published in eight languages, and he has received several awards, including two Pen Writers' Grants.

"I think that timing means a lot. Growing up in the literature as a true child of the '60s, I found that my search for an individual literary style and innovation followed my love for what was happening in jazz at the time.

"In my youth I was fortunate to have performed alongside people like Archie Shepp, Don Cherry, Alice Coltrane, and Leon Thomas. Having access to discussions about harmonics and other aspects of musical theory helped me to seek after making language do what the music was doing.

"My usage of harmonics, tonal and sonic modulation, and layers of figurative language all came from jazz (with some help of course from French Symbolists, Impressionists, and Surrealists). I have gladly given whatever I had to writing, and as a result my humanity has been greatly enhanced because of it. I feel that when I write that it is comparable to the act of prayer.

"Today I say that if only I could make language do what Gato Barbieri does in *Encuentros*, then I'll know that I finally learned how to master poetic language."

ALVIN AUBERT, Professor Emeritus of English at Wayne State University, taught creative writing and African American literature there and at Southern University and the State University of New York. He founded and edited the literary journal *Obsidian* and produced articles and reviews mainly on African American poetry. His own poetry, for which he received two awards from the National Endowment for the Arts, is collected in *Against the Blues; Feeling Through; South Louisiana: New and Selected Poems; If Winter Come: Collected Poems 1972–1992*; and *Harlem Wrestler*.

"I never set out to write a jazz poem in the sense of replicating a jazz score in its construction. Nor do I write blues poems in a replicative way. However, I usually write with an underlying sense of structure that impinges on these performance modes. Whether or not my poems touch on the subject of jazz and its matrix the blues, in writing them I usually feel the subliminal tug of a blues/jazz undercurrent, which exists for me as intimations of performance-like rhythmical strokes, the dynamics of which help shape their line patterns. Back in the sixties when I first started making poems, I found myself listening to blues and rhythm and blues recordings while writing. I began listening more deliberately after reading James Baldwin's account in his 1959 essay 'The Discovery of What It Means to Be an American,' of his listening to Bessie Smith recordings while writing in ethnic isolation in the 'alabaster landscape' of a Swiss mountain village. Baldwin was wrestling with his sense of identity as I was with mine in Scotlandville on the outskirts of Baton Rouge, Louisiana. It was there that I wrote my first publishable poems in the mid-1960s while teaching freshman composition and English literature and, at the age of thirty-seven, discovering the existence of writings by African Americans at the traditionally African American Southern University where I had been a student and where theretofore such writings had been suppressed. Both 'Bessie' and 'Bessie Smith's Funeral' were written there under these conditions, which included my discovery of the works of African American poets Sterling A. Brown and Robert Hayden, both of whom had employed blues and jazz modes in their poetry. Seldom did I write to the accompaniment of strictly instrumental performances, since the sound of the human voice in a musical rendition was as important to me motivationally as the musical score, and it still is, although I no longer feel the need to listen to actual recordings while writing, my musical sources having become internalized."

HOUSTON A. BAKER, JR., is director of the Center for the Study of Black Literature and Culture at the University of Pennsylvania. He has served as president of the Modern Language Association of America and has received a number of awards and honors, including a Guggenheim Fellowship and the Governor's Award for Excellence in the Humanities from the state of Pennsylvania. He has published numerous studies of Afro-American literature and culture, including *Black Studies, Rap, and the Academy*. His latest volume of poetry is *Blues Journeys Homes*.

"During the 1960s, black writers, musicians, and visual artists in the United States turned their backs on the bourgeois longings of immediate ancestors by picking up on the dialect, mores, rhythms, intonations, and style of the black majority. Their aim was to craft voices, scores, collages in harmony with the sounds, choruses, and everyday appearances of the black masses. Hence, unlike the venerable James Weldon Johnson or the always ambivalent and elusive Zora Neale Hurston, the black brother and sister artists of the sixties knew that dialect poetry was the only kind of poetry that truly counted (at least in their view) as *black*. Furthermore, these artists knew that only depictions of black everyday life—in all its historical and emotional fullness—could be useful in the process of *black* empowerment in America. Musicians tuned back into the folk rhythms and produced monuments of *black* sound with titles like *Freedom Suite.* The days of the Black Arts Movement were heady, full of experimental concept, institutions, dogmas, and nationalistic arbiters of taste. Today in the 1990s, the pregnant wisdom seems to be that the movement's emphasis on *blackness* represented a naive faith in genetic essentialism. That is to say, the movement misfired because it aggressively asserted that only generically endowed *blackness* could ensure nationalist and empowering forms of art. The Oedipal rage of a New Jack, 1990s generation of young Afro-Americans is apparent in such condemnations. The Black Arts Movement, of course, produced this generation. When it speaks, poses, postures, fumes, or gets seriously busy with independent cinema, performance art, or organizations of black musicians, it is always at its best when it acts like the Black Arts Movement said black artists in America should act. This is true because writers such as Sonia Sanchez, Amiri Baraka, June Jordan, musicians such as John Coltrane, orators such as Malcolm X, and filmmakers such as Melvin Van Peebles—all of whom helped to create the Black Arts in America—traveled, organized, and most all produced works of imaginative genius that forcefully actualized the tenets of the Black Arts Movement. It is never, of course, the doctrines that survive or become most important for any revolutionary artistic movement. It is the creativity, the personalities of the artists themselves, the actual works they produce that energize the lives and imaginations of audiences and followers and fellow artists for years to come. Jazz poetry, blues poetry, vernacular signifying in the arts of America were at their highest order of achievement during the Black Arts Movement. The movement did not invent these practices. There were ancestors like Langston Hughes, Sterling Brown, and many others. But the Black Arts Movement moved such creative practices to new heights, creating dream variations and blue innuendos that could not have been envisioned by the black bourgeoisie just a few years before the sixties. It is a basic and fundamental truth of the arts in America that in order to be a *black* artist, your work must begin with the blues. While it may find a middle passage in jazz, there is a circle of energy that brings it all back around one more time. It is a basic and fundamental truth of the arts in America that in order to be a *black* artist, your work must end with the blues."

DOROTHY BARRESI is the author of *All of the Above*, which was published as part of the Barnard New Women Poets Series. She has published in *Agni, Poetry, Ploughshares, Parnassus, Denver Quarterly, Michigan Quarterly*, and other magazines. She has also been a Fellow at the Fine Arts Work Center in Provincetown and is currently an associate professor of English at California State University, Northridge.

"I've long been fascinated with popular culture in America as a mirror for our private dreams and sorrows—a fun house mirror, at times, it's true, distorting, but giving back something we recognize and respond to deeply in ourselves. Music is part of all that, and in 'Venice Beach: Brief Song' I've tried to bring together the jazzy insistence of a place and a time that is both liberating and dangerous, a place that makes us wish for escape, 'flying and flying and flying.' Of course the speaker knows that she cannot really escape, though there are all sorts of attempts at it going on in the poem in the references to crystal meth, Sufis on rollerskates, rockets, etc., so the prayer she offers up at the end is sadly comic, I think. As for the appearance of Bix Beiderbecke and 'I'm Coming Virginia' at the end of such a contemporary poem, well, I hope that it unites this particular crazy time and place—Venice, California, circa now—with a larger, American yearning for identity and reassurance that stretches backwards and forwards throughout the twentieth century. By the way, the Capitol Records Building, while not *really* visible from Venice Beach, is one of my favorite images in the poem, as it was built to resemble a stack of records!—a punk Guggenheim in the center of Hollywood."

PAUL BEATTY is the author of *Big Bank Take Little Bank* and *Joker, Joker, Deuce*.

JOHN BERRYMAN (1914–1972) was the author of many books of poetry, including *Homage to Mistress Bradstreet, Delusions, etc.*, and *The Dream Songs*; his *Collected Poems 1937–1971* was published posthumously in 1989. He was also the author of several books of prose, including *The Arts of Reading; Recovery;* and *The Freedom of the Poet*. His many awards and prizes included the National Book Award, the Bollingen Prize, and the Pulitzer Prize for Poetry.

GWENDOLYN BROOKS is the author of numerous books of poetry, including *A Street in Bronzeville; Blacks; Winnie*; and *Gottschalk and the Grande Tarantelle*. She has received more than fifty honorary degrees as well as numerous awards and prizes, including the American Academy of Arts and Letters Award, a National Endowment for the Arts Fellowship, two Guggenheim Fellowships, and the Pulitzer Prize for Poetry. She is currently the Poet Laureate of Illinois.

ARTHUR BROWN (1947–1982) published one chapbook of poetry during his lifetime—*Song of the Sly Mongoose*—but *River Styx* magazine later published a special issue titled *A Trumpet in the Morning*, which featured about half of his collected poems. Another posthumous collection, *Mississippi River Poems: Selected and New Writing*, appeared in 1990. His presence is still strongly felt among the poets from the St. Louis area.

CHRISTOPHER BUCKLEY has published seven books of poetry, most recently *Dark Matter* and *A Short History of Light*. He has also published a book of creative nonfiction, *Cruising State: Growing Up in Southern California* and edited both *On the Poetry of Philip Levine: Stranger to Nothing* and *What Will Suffice: The Ars Poetica in Contemporary American Poetry*. Currently, he is completing a new book of poems, *Camino Cielo*. He teaches creative writing at West Chester University in Pennsylvania.

"I can enjoy a little Ornette Coleman, and certainly someone he influenced, Pat Metheny. But a lot of fusion leaves me cold. My real base, my passion for jazz goes back to the big bands and to folks like Ben Webster, Coleman Hawkins, early Coltrane, and Sonny Rollins.

"My father was a DJ, and growing up in the late '40s and early '50s, I was listening to recordings of Glenn Miller and Bunny Berrigan, Jo Stafford, June Christy, and Julie London long before I knew one kind of music from another. In the car or at home the radio was always on and later the Hi Fi; that music was there day and night. And it's been with me since, consciously or not, almost a memory from another life—which, at forty-six, is, I guess, about what it is, and so the requisite nostalgia and moody bass beat in the blood backing up the lines.

"'Nostalgia,' from my first book, is concerned with our place in time as a generation—baby boomers we were called—on the edge of our grandparents' generation from the turn of the century, our parents' generation from WWII and our own, the atomic age. I wanted to preserve a little of that more innocent time, an age given to silky melodies, vocal stylings, and sentiment largely gone forever now. And so a more steady or pensive rhythm in this poem than might be associated with a 'jazz' poem—more of a ballad/big band sound in those lines, to my ear.

"I didn't really listen to Ben Webster until the late '70s when the poet Peter Everwine introduced me to his recordings. I was knocked out from the start with the lingering textures and overlays of notes. The soulful slides and flutters, the smooth syncopations he coaxed out of his sax, the pathos he fleshed out from a melody.

"For 'Playing for Time' I tried for a more upbeat tempo, a more conscious jazz rhythm to keep the syntax and imagery moving. I wanted the voice to improvise a little, run over and skip the end stops and predictable phrasings. The poem tries to have lighter, charged riffs work out the weight of its subject.

"It's a bit of an ars poetica too—art for the sake of art—pointing out how undervalued and yet life sustaining art is, music or writing. It is an occasional poem in that the poet Gary Young and I came across these street musicians one day in San Francisco—best I've ever heard. They were just getting along with what they had on hand for the sake of the music basically. It was clear they weren't making any money despite the exceptional quality of their playing. They gave their gift for anyone with ears—the music had to be its own reward. After a while, Gary and I headed down the street a bit saddened that those guys were so great and so overlooked but lifted in spirit, feeling a bit richer, momentarily elevated by the upbeat swing and electricity in the music of our lives.

"One of the last times I saw my father, he had found a newly mixed recording of Artie Shaw and his band with a young Mel Tormé doing the vocals. It took him back, and at his house over dinner that night it was clear he was somewhere else. For these poems, for others, I hope the music is at the base of things, and I hope it always takes me somewhere."

MICHAEL CASTRO is the founder of River Styx, a literary organization based in St. Louis, which has, since 1975, sponsored the River Styx at Duff's reading series and published the magazine *River Styx*. Castro also hosts the *Poetry Beat* radio program on station KDHX-FM in St. Louis. Long interested in poetry as a performance art, he has worked over the years with many jazz musicians—among them David Hines, Marty Ehrlich, J. D. Parran, and the groups the Human Arts Ensemble and Harmony. His published works include *The Kokopilau Cycle; Ghost Highways and Other Homes; Cracks; (US);* and the literary history *Interpreting the Indian: Twentieth Century Poets and the Native American.* He currently teaches at Lindenwood College.

"My first direct experience of the coincidence of poetry and jazz came in 1967. I was at a club called Slug's in the East Village listening to a startling call and response exchange between saxophonist Pharoah Sanders and vocalist Leon Thomas. The two seemed to swap instruments—vocal utterances spit out of Pharoah's soul-piercing sax and Thomas's voice became an answering horn blowing from the depths. The whole audience was plugged in, electrified. The piece ended and a guy sitting in front of me got up and started reciting one of my favorite poems, Garcia Lorca's 'Sleepwalker's

Ballad'—'Verde, que tu quiero verde / Verde viento. Verdes ramas . . .' ('Green, how much I want you green. / Green wind. Green branches'). Out of left field as it was, it seemed so translogically right—not so much as a commentary on what we had just heard (though that too), but as a continuation, an extension of it. The guy was simply riding the wave.

"It was Pound who urged the poet to know another art form intimately, and I found myself following his advice, hanging out with jazz musician friends, blowing my art with theirs. The exchanges always taught me something about my own poems, but also about what we reverently called 'the music.' This was not so much the sounds played, the words uttered, but the impulse behind them, the inexpressible 'procreant urge' in our individual and collective souls that we were reaching for, trying to articulate. Muse. Music. The music was at once product, source, creator, teacher. A healing, unifying force, it was beyond any person, any planet, any material thing.

"In 1978, I was leading a poetry workshop for fifth graders. We were doing an exercise, creating 'naming poems' that followed a formula of ancient Egyptian god-naming. We composed lists of people we knew, coupling each person's name with a phrase starting with 'the one' and concluding with what we saw as a telling characteristic of that person: Allison, the one with the silky black hair; Tyrone, the silent one, etc. When it came to me, the class came up with: 'Mr. Castro, the one with the rhythm.' I was awed, humbled, sensing they had penetrated to the core of what I—and the poetry I was trying to teach them—was all about. They had been touched by the movement beyond words. *The music.* Now it was theirs."

RICHARD CECIL is the author of *Einstein's Brain* and *Alcatraz*. He currently teaches at Indiana University.

"I've been singing the blues since I was born, with less justification than most. I've led a pretty lucky life. But when I think about it, I can dredge up misery from memory and add it to present misery to fill out the measure. When I wrote 'Richard's Blues' I was working far from home, a state away from my wife and cats, staying up most nights reading *The Complete Works of Shakespeare* cover to cover to profit from my insomnia. The poem started to be about that, but another night of insomnia, when I was fifteen and in love for the first time, desperately crept in and took over. It was a hot night in Baltimore. I lay in bed with my transistor radio tuned to *Hotrod's Rocketship Show* on WEBB, Baltimore's black station. Every show began with Ray Charles playing solo piano while Hotrod talked about the blind piano player from Georgia. I loved Ray Charles—his songs crossed over to the top forty stations I listened to during the daytime—but this night his work didn't just *amuse* me, it *helped* me, the way Shakespeare did, twenty-five years later. Ray Charles was the first poet who changed my life; Shakespeare was the last. So, though I started 'Richard's Blues' with misery in mind, the poem ended up more as a tribute to geniuses who turned their misery into art that turned my nights of insomnia into deep, rich memories, better than the dreams I missed by not sleeping."

KAREN CHASE has had poems appear in many magazines and journals, including the *Gettysburg Review, Another Chicago Magazine*, and *Shenandoah*; she has also been anthologized in *Yellow Silk, Erotic Arts and Letters*, and *Under One Roof*. She has received numerous grants and awards from such places as the Witter Bynner Foundation for Poetry and the Public Welfare Foundation, and recently she received a Rockefeller Bellagio Fellowship. She is the poet-in-residence at New York Hospital–Cornell Medical Center, where she teaches writing to psychiatric patients.

"Jazz. It's the back and forth, back and forth of it that's great. It's the back and forth, back and forth, back and back and forth of it that's great. It's our collaborative art. You play together, you play separate, the non-lonely art form. Jazz is just the right distance away, close to the insides, awakens response."

JANE COOPER is the author of four books of poems, most recently *Green Notebook; Winter Road;* and *Scaffolding: Selected Poems.* Among her numerous honors are the Lamont Award for her first collection and the 1985 Maurice English Poetry Award for *Scaffolding*. She taught for many years at Sarah Lawrence College, where she helped to invent the writing program.

"I lived as a child in a rural area outside Jacksonville, Florida, during the Depression. Most of my classmates in the local elementary school were children of shrimp fishermen or white sharecroppers, whose bleached-out faces spoke of bottomless poverty. 'School closed early' during those years (it also opened late) because the state couldn't afford to pay the teachers. I left that school when I was nine but could never forget the children. I wanted to write about them, but it seemed I had lost their language. The blues form gave me access again to something like the sound of their lives.

"'Wanda's Blues' is dedicated to my sister-in-law, Joan H. Cooper, who has worked with and on behalf of children in several different cultures."

HART CRANE (1899–1933) was the author of *White Buildings, The Bridge*, and *Collected Poems*. Posthumous collections include *Ten Unpublished Poems* and *The Complete Poems and Selected Letters and Prose*, which provides this statement:

"The poetry of negation is beautiful—alas, too dangerously so for one of my mind. But I am trying to break away from it. Perhaps this is useless, perhaps it is silly—but one *does* have joys. The vocabulary of damnations and prostrations has been developed at the expense of these other moods, however, so that it is hard to dance in proper measure. Let us invent an idiom for the proper transposition of jazz into words! Something clean, sparkling, elusive!"

STANLEY CROUCH, who used to write regularly for the *Village Voice*, has published in many magazines and journals, including *Harper's,* the *New York Times, Vogue, Downbeat*, the *Amsterdam News*, and the *New Republic*, where he is also a contributing editor. He has served as artistic consultant for jazz programming at Lincoln Center since 1987 and is a founder of the jazz department, known as Jazz at Lincoln Center. His collection of essays and reviews, *Notes of a Hanging Judge*, was nominated for an award in criticism by the National Book Critics Circle and was selected by the Encyclopedia Britannica Yearbook as the best book of essays published in 1990. He is in the process of completing many large projects about jazz.

"At the time that I was writing the poems included in this collection, my mind was set on the rhythms of jazz. I wanted to make the lines SWING, which is to say that I sought the kind of motion that one hears in the music of jazz. It had to do with finding out how to summon either the particular kind of percussive accenting basic to jazz rhythm or, from the other side, the kind of dancing, floating melodies improvised by those jazz musicians who combine singing with swinging. Studying blues lyrics was especially important because there were often writing secrets found in the best of them, where the pains of loss fused with the gains of love.

"As for construction, I was concerned with form in a very open sense. I wanted to build those poems on image and emotion, letting the line stretch out in varied lengths while shooting for the organic effect that arrives when one sweats enough over the work to give it a feeling of 'natural' inevitability. Much of what I considered 'natural' came from those whose work I took most seriously. I was influenced, above all others, by William Butler Yeats and LeRoi Jones. Yeats had a modern but ancient lyricism that was tragic at the core, so merciless in its sniffing out of human foulness but so affirmative in its refusal to throw aside the multi-directional affections that were experienced by a rich and detailing consciousness. Jones, before he turned in his universal feeling for an ethnic costume, had a superb grasp of what I call, in jazz, 'industrial lyricism,' the imposition of song upon the hard, technological momentum of the city. I was also taken by the poetry of Robert Hayden who, at his best, pulled together that tragic lyricism with the city strut of skyscrapers, plate glass, mass transit, electricity, and metal bent to human will.

"However much I loved the work of others, I think I had something of my own, a personal way to get my heart and mind on the page. But sheer expression wasn't my central concern. I always wanted technique. I believed that too much of what was being written during those hairy days of ethnic outcry amounted to a whole lot of shaking but little singing. The black nationalist movement of that time soon seemed to me largely no more than a segregated playground, not a ring in which one took on the masters.

"The tracks of my life have led me away from poetry. I now use all that I learned then and have absorbed since in order to give some sort of song to my prose. Yet I will never forget how good it was to sit up all night reading the work of masters and hot contemporary talents, gleaning what I could, then diving into the infinite white ocean of the empty page and trying to stroke my way toward something I wouldn't be ashamed of calling a poem. No matter the lumps, there is always a delicious sting to the memory of the struggle for aesthetic clarity, the attempt to make all that is human fold in upon itself for the wholeness upon which we base all of our myths of civilization."

E. E. CUMMINGS (1894–1962) published more than twenty-five collections of poetry during his lifetime, and his *Complete Poems 1913–1962* appeared posthumously.

JAMES CUSHING is the author of *You and the Night and the Music*. While teaching at the University of California–Irvine and Pasadena City College, he hosted "The Marriage of Heaven and Hell," a poetry-and-music program on Pacifica Radio, and directed the award-winning Al's Bar poetry readings series. He teaches at California State Polytechnic University at Pomona and Cuesta College and hosts jazz programs on National Public Radio.

"Since 1977, I've been writing poems based on American popular songs that have entered the jazz repertoire. I am not a jazz musician myself, but I find jazz central to my experience of art. When a great improvisor essays a tune, he transforms its universal romance by means of his own temperament and experience. This transformation of a universal theme into a personal idiom strikes me as a useful, attractive metaphor for aesthetic activity. My experience has been that life, in Carolyn Forché's words, is 'complex beyond comprehension,' yet ordered by language and traditions within, beneath, or adjacent to that complexity. I would like to get some of the feeling of jazz into my poetry without aping it in any surface way, being true to my own experience while acknowledging what is greater than my own experience—history, destiny, the unchanging facts of the human heart."

ROBERT DANA retired recently from full-time teaching after forty years at Cornell College. His most recent book is *Yes, Everything*, and his honors include the Delmore Schwartz Memorial Prize for Poetry and two National Endowment for the Arts Fellowships.

"I don't think I can improve on anything the critic Edward Brunner said about my poems in a recent review, so I take the liberty of quoting him. 'A Dana poem seems not crafted but improvised. Yet it is about as "effortless" as a jazz solo that brings to bear years of experience. You hold your breath as the poem takes place, wondering if it will stay in one piece line by line, and if it will tie up with a twist at the end. The mystery is that Dana manages to appear so offhand, so fresh, yet still retains his authority.'

"Brunner is right. I work improvisationally. I hang out in the empty space of the page on the wings of a good ground rhythm, the music of the words, and the faith that I can make it fly. I believe the poem is always right there, in front of our eyes, nothing too humble—I have only to have my blessing on to get it to sing."

FRANK MARSHALL DAVIS (1905–1987) was a poet and journalist whose books of poetry include *Black Man's Verse, I Am the American Negro, Through Sepia Eyes*, and *47th Street: Poems*. He was also the author of an autobiography, *Livin' the Blues: Memoirs of a Black Journalist and Poet*, edited by John Edgar Tidwell, who is currently editing his collected poems. In *Livin' the Blues*, Davis writes,

"During the same period that I was acquiring initial sex misinformation, I became conscious of the blues and evolving jazz. It's quite logical to discuss sex and jazz together; the music had developed for dancing, and people went to shindigs for close contact with members of the opposite sex which, with luck and opportunity, might end up in bed. Further, jazz meant both a kind of music as well as the sex act itself. It was obvious what the composer had in mind when he wrote 'Jazz Me Blues.'"

THULANI N. DAVIS is the author of several books, including the poetry collection *Playing the Changes*, the novel *1959*, and *Malcolm X: The Great Photographs*. She also writes journalism and plays. She is currently living in Brooklyn, New York.

"The great challenge of writing about improvised music is to give a sense of being 'in the moment.' That is how the music is created and yet it is the hardest part of writing any poetry. I try to capture the improbabilities that somehow seem right when the music is played."

DIANE DI PRIMA has written more than twenty-five books of poetry, including *The Selected Poems of Diane di Prima*. She is also the author of several plays and novels.

"The requirements of our life is the form of our art."

MARK DOTY has written four books of poems, including *Atlantis* and *My Alexandria*, which won the National Book Critics Circle Award and the Los Angeles Times Book Prize for 1994 and which was a finalist for the National Book Award. He has received fellowships from the National Endowment for the Arts and the Guggenheim, Ingram Merrill, and Rockefeller foundations. He lives in Provincetown, Massachusetts.

"'Almost Blue' is a poem about loving Chet Baker's magnetic alloy of energy and damage, and wanting to be able to 'sing' with something approaching his extraordinary phrasing."

RITA DOVE is the author of several books of poetry, including *Thomas and Beulah*, *Grace Notes*, and *Selected Poems*. She has received many awards and honors, including a National Endowment for the Arts Fellowship, a Guggenheim Fellowship, and the Pulitzer Prize for Poetry.

HENRY DUMAS (1934–1968) was the author of several books of poetry and fiction, including *Ark of Bones*, *Rope of Wind*, *Play Ebony Play Ivory*, and *Jonoah and the Green Stone*. Two other works, *Goodbye, Sweetwater* and *Knees of a Natural Man: The Selected Poetry of Henry Dumas*, were edited by Eugene B. Redmond and appeared posthumously.

CORNELIUS EADY is the author of five books of poetry: *Kartunes; Victims of the Latest Dance Craze* (winner of the 1985 Lamont Prize from the American Academy of Poets); *The Gathering of My Name* (nominated for the 1992 Pulitzer Prize for Poetry); *You Don't Miss Your Water*; and *The Autobiography of a Jukebox*. He is the recipient of a grant from the National Endowment for the Arts, a Guggenheim Fellowship, a Lila Wallace–Reader's Digest Traveling Scholarship to Tougaloo College in Mississippi, a Rockefeller Foundation Fellowship to Bellagio, Italy, and the Prairie Schooner Strousee Award. His work appears in many journals and magazines and was featured on National Public Radio's *Morning Edition*. He is currently Associate Professor of English and director of the Poetry Center at SUNY Stony Brook.

JAMES A. EMANUEL is the author of eleven volumes of poems, including *Whole Grain: Collected Poems, 1958–1989; De la Rage au Coeur*; and *Blues in Black and White*. His many prose works include *Langston Hughes* and *Dark Symphony: Negro Literature in America* (with Theodore Gross).

"*Poetics*, says one dictionary, takes a singular verb and deals with 'the nature, forms, and laws of poetry.' J. Paul Hunter, in his *The Norton Introduction to Poetry*, cannot reduce his veteran knowledge of poetics to a certainty.

"After nearly forty years of writing poetry, I know that poetics *is*, echoing the fifth-century B.C. conclusion of Parmenides, 'Being is.' The NATURE of poetry, details aside, is this: aesthetic unity. In the visible world, that unity simply *is*. The multiple FORMS of poetry are faithful to its nature in embodying that pleasurable unity. The omnipresence of symmetry around us reveals aesthetic intent in the cosmos. The LAWS of poetry, like man-made laws, are just and tolerable only when they clarify and safeguard the principles manifest in the nature and forms of its being.

"The danger in established poetics resembles the danger in human laws: the tyranny of definitions stamped 'immutable and reverend' in defiance of the commandments of changing times. But just as we must concentrate upon purpose, not danger, a working poet, Parmenidean in trust, can only *be*, be what he is: one who creates suitable forms to express the nature and truth of his experience. Those forms, Yeatsian terrible or Keatsian lovely in aesthetic appeal, bare-knuckle or compassionate in social thrust, need obey only laws that nourish a harmony of words and sensations hopefully as life-like as remembered tunes, as pleasing as comfortable shoes in good weather."

MARTÍN ESPADA is the author of four books: *The Immigrant Iceboy's Bolero; Trumpets from the Islands of Their Eviction; Rebellion Is the Circle of a Lover's Hands (Rebelión es el Giro de Manos del Amante);* and *City of Coughing and Dead Radiators.* He is also editor of the anthology *Poetry Like Bread: Poets of the Political Imagination from Curbstone Press.* He has been awarded two fellowships from the National Endowment for the Arts, a Massachusetts Artists Fellowship, and the PEN/Revson Foundation Fellowship, as well as the Patterson Poetry Prize. Many of his poems arise from his work experiences, ranging from bouncer in a bar to tenant lawyer. Espada currently teaches in the English Department at the University of Massachusetts–Amherst.

"The two poems which represent my work in this anthology—'Majeski Plays the Saxophone' and 'Shaking Hands with Mongo'—are built on the same foundations: image and music.

"Pablo Neruda is one of my primary influences, and that influence manifests itself in several ways, including the emphasis on the image. There is a deliberate confluence of naturalistic detail and surreal observation, documentary one moment and dreamlike the next, which indicate in both poems a movement into a world which is familiar, yet ultimately beyond our understanding.

"The two poems are also founded, of course, on jazz. I write about jazz the way other poets write about paintings in museums. In each poem, the pace and texture of the language attempt to reflect the instrument played by the central character, whether the harsh, yet meditative saxophone in 'Majeski,' or the insistently percussive conga of 'Mongo.' The suffering and celebration in each poem find natural expression through metaphors of music.

"'Majeski' is based on a patient incarcerated in a maximum security mental hospital in Wisconsin, who came to my attention while I was working as a patient rights advocate in that state during the late 1970s. His name has been changed for reasons of confidentiality. The poem does not posit an explanation of the man or his actions but serves as testimony to what was seen and heard in that secret and forbidding place.

"'Mongo' is based on two great Afro-Cuban musicians: Mongo Santamaría and Chano Pozo. I did shake hands with Mongo, and at that moment thought of Chano, who was actually murdered in a bar more than four decades ago; 'Manteca' was his most famous song. The Spanish words in the poem are present for sound texture but also for fidelity: after all, this was the language of the music and the musicians. This is a poem of homage but also of haunting, praising the music as a rich source of cultural identity, yet mourning the musicians, like Chano, whose lives reflect the realities of this community.

"This, then, is the reward for working in the vein of jazz poetry: that, like a jazz funeral, it may encompass the intimate and the inexplicable, the celebratory and the tragic, the roughest and smoothest of textures, the range of rhythms from quickening to dying."

DAVE ETTER is the author of many books of poetry, including *Central Standard Time: New and Selected Poems* and *Well You Needn't: The Thelonious Monk Poems*.

"The three poems of mine included in this anthology are from *Well You Needn't: The Thelonious Monk Poems*, published in 1975. I completed them and seventeen others over a six-month period when I was collecting and playing Monk albums, almost exclusively. In these poems I never attempted to put words to the music. What I did was to play a particular piece, say, 'In Walked Bud,' over and over until Monk's intoxicating sounds triggered an image or images and the rhythms suggested a form or structure for a poem. The words and the lines often came quickly, but I revised a good deal when stronger impulses arrived. I consider my Monk poems to be experimental, even surreal at times, but never obscure.

"I have been a very big jazz fan for as far back as I can remember: since Ellington, since Basie, since Goodman, since Artie Shaw, since Herman, since Kenton, since bebop and Bird, Dizzy, Bud Powell, et al. When I began to write poetry seriously in my mid-twenties I would do so while listening to jazz, and it just developed into a habit, one that I practice today. Jazz helps me with the problems I might have with structure, rhythm, sound, tempo, harmony, repetition, word choice, line length, and precision. It also has taught me about the advantages of using simplicity and common everyday speech and how important emotion and feeling are in any work of art.

"The above is not to say that my poetry has not gained a great deal from reading other poets. I have tried to read them all, including foreign poets, in translation. At the present time, the wonderful blues-drenched poems of Langston Hughes have been occupying much of my reading time. I should also point out that in writing and publishing twenty-two volumes of poetry it would be difficult for me to find a poem of mine that wasn't in some way a 'jazz' poem."

MARI EVANS is the author of four volumes of poetry: *I Am a Black Woman; Singing Black; Nightstar;* and *A Dark and Splendid Mass*. In addition, she is the author of four children's books, several performed theater pieces, and two musicals, and the editor of *Black Women Writers (1950–1980): A Critical Evaluation*.

SARAH WEBSTER FABIO (1928–1979) was a poet and a teacher. Her books include *Saga of a Black Man; A Mirror A Soul;* and *Black Talk: Soul, Shield, and Sword*. She also made two sound recordings, *Boss Soul* and *Soul Ain't, Soul Is*. In the introduction to her book *JuJus and Jubilees*, a collection which included "For Louis Armstrong, A Ju-Ju," Fabio wrote:

"Black Poems have a relation in kind to Western Poetry which Black Jazz—Black Music—has to what is known as Western Classical Music. They are both vanguard art forms—always way out front, out there all by themselves. To reduce the mysticism which obstructs communication in an age of technology by those who are not attuned to the spiritual side of human nature—those who indeed step to a different drummer from the poet—it is possible, as I have done, to ascribe and describe and illustrate by example the functional aspects of this craft."

THORPE FEIDT, whose painting appears on the cover, teaches painting and drawing at Montserrat College of Art in Beverly, Massachusetts, and a course in the humanities at the University of New Hampshire at Manchester. He has had solo exhibitions in many cities, including New York, Philadelphia, and Boston. He has worked in theater and film as an actor, director, and photographer, and has edited several literary magazines. He is currently completing "The Ambiguities," a series of 333 paintings, as well as a novel entitled *The Leibniz Papers*.

"Jazz has been the companion of my painting ever since high school. At the same time I was experiencing the wonder and enthusiasm inspired by the prospect of a lifetime devoted wholly to art, I was listening with equal excitement to Thelonious Monk (*Monk's Music*, which Riverside records had just released) and discovering Miles and Sonny Rollins as well, along with Clark Terry, Milt Jackson, Mingus, Mulligan and Baker, Al and Zoot. Today, close to forty years later, most aspects of my life have changed completely, but not this: I still paint with enthusiasm and wonder, and I still listen to jazz.

"I work to make paintings that *swing*, that come alive through the motion they contain, not through the static shapes of objects depicted. I work to make dynamic interchanges take place—where elements pulse and vibrate against each other, where improvised, freely painted areas break off from insistent, regularly accented beats, where colors clash in dissonance or flow together in harmony, where lines assert themselves as gesture and direction, and space itself takes an active role, talking back, loud, to the forms that occupy it. The whole is articulated by feeling and intuition—by 'insight, not eyesight,' as the painter Paul Scott used to insist—not by planning beforehand, and it must be this way, since the *point* of the thing is for feeling to enter the painting as a vital presence, and to bring with it that indefinable but absolutely real entity, soul.

"Now, jazz doesn't have to be avant-garde to swing, and if the look my paintings end up with is 'modern,' the tradition behind them is old as the hills. Thales of Miletus, one of the Seven Sages of ancient Greece, might never have heard the music of the Sphere, but more than twenty-five hundred years ago he made an observation, so it's said, which puts him high up there near the top on my list of all-time heroes. Having noticed that Magnesian stone was capable of moving iron, he concluded 'that the soul was something kinetic' and 'intermingled with the universe.' (He also is supposed to have said, 'All things are full of gods.') Thus, everything, animate and inanimate, *is* animate. (*Anima* in Latin means 'soul.') For me, these are not empty words or dry bits of long-dead history; they are the living expression of a presence I daily feel moving at the center of my experience. And the *sound* of that motion, for me, is jazz: it's Sonny Stitt and Gene Ammons trading breaks on 'Blues Up and Down'; it's Art Baron on trombone, soloing on 'Blues in the 2%' with the Frank Wess orchestra; it's Monk at the keyboard, working over 'Lulu's Back in Town.' And these moments have vivid equivalents for me in painting: the speed and crackle of de Kooning's 'Gotham News'; the emotional richness and narrative urgency of Kandinsky's great 'Improvisations' of 1913; the jagged rhythms and sudden shifts in scale and color of George McNeil's 'Summer Dress,' at once fierce and humorous. All these works—in sound and paint—speak to the core of reality I feel in the world and which I seek to celebrate as an artist."

SASCHA FEINSTEIN is the author of *Jazz Poetry: From the 1920's to the Present* and *A Bibliographic Guide to Jazz Poetry*. His poems and essays about jazz have appeared in a variety of publications, including the *Southern Review, New England Review*, and *North American Review*. His awards include the 1995 Writers' Exchange Program Award for poetry. Formerly the director of the Indiana University Writers' Conference, he currently teaches creative writing and literature at Lycoming College.

"'Sonnets for Stan Gage' was written in tribute to one of the great Indianapolis drummers, who spent the last years of his life in Bloomington, where we became friends. A performer with many terrific musicians, Stan did not record very much, but he can be heard on the guitarist Royce Campbell's CD, *Elegy for a Friend*.

"'Christmas Eve' features a very famous incident in jazz history, one that's still documented on the Prestige CD, *Miles Davis and the Modern Jazz Giants*. In Dan Morgenstern's notes for Miles Davis's *Chronicle: The Complete Prestige Recordings*, he writes that 'Too much may have been made of the supposed tension between Miles and Monk on this date.' But if I'm guilty of exploiting that tension, then the producers of *Chronicle* are guilty of ignoring Miles's wish: the whole argument has been omitted from this boxed set. I think Miles would've disapproved."

WILLIAM FORD has published poems in many magazines and journals, including *Poetry,* the *Iowa Review*, and *Poet and Critic*. He has also been a finalist for several national book contests. He currently lives in Iowa City.

"Why is it that the blues aren't depressing when they've become The Blues? Enter the problem of form, what makes participation and release possible. As Walker Percy said in a more philosophical context, the difference between an alienated person and a person who contemplates alienation is immense. The contemplative has more freedom of movement, is not dominated by the raw feeling. That's why Kafka could read 'The Metamorphosis' to his friends with tears and falling-down laughter. That's why Billie Holiday could sing 'Fine and Mellow' while smiling so sweetly to Count Basie.

"Poetry and jazz make sounds and move in time. Both tend to be confessional and celebrational. Jazz is America's chamber music, the great leveler and lifter. Poetry uses language harder, more compressively; jazz, sound.

"If all art 'aspires to the condition of music,' it's natural that poetry should experiment with various kinds of rhythm and sound. Some poets use words so as to sound like Monk or Coleman or Davis. (Because he's current again, try Kerouac.) It's a kind of translation, surely. A poem may hint at a Monkish music, but can it do much more than that before it competes with its original as pure music? The attempt honors the source. And don't forget that Ellington knew and used his Shakespeare."

NIKKI GIOVANNI has published several books of poetry, including *Spin a Soft Black Song: Poems for Children; My House; The Women and the Men;* and *Those Who Ride the*

Night Winds. She has also published several books of nonfiction and made sound recordings. Her latest book is titled *Racism 101.*

MATTHEW GRAHAM is the author of two books of poetry, *New World Architecture* and *1946*. He teaches at the University of Southern Indiana and co-directs the Rope Walk Writers Retreat in New Harmony, Indiana.

"American poetry tries to reflect the rhythms and the music that are inherent in the gumbo of American speech. Jazz seems to do the same. It is fitting that they be joined."

SAM GREENLEE has published three volumes of poetry, *Blues for an African Princess; Ammunition!;* and *Be-Bop Man, Be-Bop Woman,* his first publication since 1976. His first novel, *The Spook Who Sat by the Door,* is an international prize-winning best–seller that was translated into six languages. Greenlee has been an All-American middle distance runner; an Infantry Officer during the Korean War; a Foreign Service Officer; a college professor; a radio talk show host; a poet, novelist, playwright; a screenwriter, director, producer, and filmmaker. More recently, he has been a taxi driver in Chicago; a Gypsy cab driver in Harlem and the South Bronx; and a farm laborer and construction worker in the south of Spain.

"My chief literary influences are Charlie Parker, Lester Young, Miles Davis, and Billie Holiday. As a writer, I consider myself a jazz musician whose instrument is a type-writer" (*Blues for an African Princess,* back cover).

JOY HARJO has published four books of poetry, including *She Had Some Horses* and the award-winning *In Mad Love and War. Secrets from the Center of the World* is a collaboration with photographer/astronomer Stephen Strom. She is currently a professor in the creative writing program at the University of New Mexico. Her many awards include the Josephine Miles Award, the William Carlos Williams Award, the Delmore Schwartz Award, the American Book Award, and the 1990 American Indian Distinguished Achievement Award. Harjo also plays the saxophone with her band, Poetic Justice.

"Once I was so small that I could barely peer over the top of the back seat of the black Cadillac my father polished and tuned daily; I wanted to see everything. It was around the time I acquired language, or even before that time when something happened that changed my relationship to the spin of the world. My concept of language, of what was possible with music, was charged by this revelatory moment. It changed even the way I looked at the sun. This suspended integer of time probably escaped ordinary notice in my parents' universe, which informed most of my vision in the ordinary world. They were still omnipresent gods. We were driving somewhere in Tulsa, the northern border of the Creek Nation. I don't know where we were going or where we had been, but I know the sun was boiling the asphalt, the car windows open for any breeze as I stood on tiptoes on the floorboard behind my father, a handsome god who smelled of Old Spice, whose slick black hair was always impeccably groomed, his clothes perfectly creased and ironed. The radio was on. I loved the radio, jukeboxes, or any magic thing containing music even then.

"I wonder now what signaled this moment, a loop of time that on first glance could be any place in time. I became acutely aware of the line the jazz trumpeter was playing (a sound I later associated with Miles Davis). I didn't know the word jazz or trumpet, or the concepts. I don't know how to say it, with what sounds or words, but in that confluence of hot southern afternoon, in the breeze of aftershave and humidity, I followed that sound to the beginning, to the place of the birth of sound. I was suspended in whirling stars, a moon to which I'd traveled often by then. I grieved my parents' failings, my own life which I saw stretched the length of that rhapsody.

"My rite of passage into the world of humanity occurred then, via jazz. The music made a startling bridge between familiar and strange lands, an appropriate vehicle, for though the music is predominately west African in concept, with European associations, jazz was influenced by the Creek (or Muscogee) people, for we were there when jazz was born. I recognized it, that humid afternoon in my formative years, as a way to speak beyond the confines of ordinary language. I still hear it."

MICHAEL S. HARPER has published several books of poems, including *Dear John, Dear Coltrane; History Is Your Own Heartbeat; Nightmare Begins Responsibility; Images of Kin;* and *Healing Song for the Inner Ear*. He holds the Israel J. Kapstein Professorship of English at Brown University, where he currently teaches.

SEAN HARVEY was born in Berea, Kentucky, and was raised in Chicago. He has worked in the past as a freelance musician and has lived in various parts of the country and in the Caribbean. He now lives in New York City, writes poetry, and works for the United Nations Development Program.

"I think that there is a way in which Clifford Brown is my main poetic influence. I've always admired his intricacy, sense of form and frightening energy above just about all other artists. There are also some definite connections between the processes I learned as a musician and those I am learning as a poet. Despite this, I have been slow to write about music. One reason is that so much has already been written about jazz, and I have had the great fortune (and in one sense misfortune) to study with perhaps the two best poets of jazz, Yusef Komunyakaa and William Matthews. It has thus taken awhile to stake out untilled territory. My poem in this anthology is an attempt to find such a place. While most jazz poetry speaks of jazz greats that have already spent decades of painstaking work to get to where they are, I hoped to write more about the learning process and the pitfalls of jazz. There are literally thousands of scrubs like myself with a deep and abiding love for the art form, and their lives are in their own way as fascinating and poignant as those of the giants of jazz. 'Vivas for those who suck!'"

JOE HEITHAUS is learning about jazz in Bloomington, Indiana, where he received an M.F.A. in poetry and is completing his Ph.D. in American literature. His poems have appeared in the *New England Review, Antioch Review*, and other magazines.

"Jazz has the power to transform, deconstruct. I smile when it surprises, when it makes an old tune new. It can be ironic, rebellious, even revolutionary. While I write a dissertation on Amiri Baraka and other poets whose work transformed itself during the revolutions in the 1960s, I see the influence this music has had on our culture. Poets learn from jazz. Its rhythms mimic our talk, its improvisations reveal our culture's impatience with set forms, its music, grown out of African American traditions, crosses boundaries of race and class by appealing to a sense of play, a joy of discovery common to everyone."

DAVID HENDERSON's books of poetry include *Felix of the Silent Forest, De Mayor of Harlem,* and *The Low East.*

"Poetry is the people's form of expression. Poetry is the basis of all literary forms, and the germ of a wide ranging array of artistic expressions. Poetry embodies the creative principle. That's why the study and practice of poetry is so important. Not necessarily to turn out poets, but to develop creative and critical approaches to problems and technique that can be brought to bear on every profession, job, activity people engage in. . . . Poetry is published in the heart, not necessarily in a journal or a book, for the majority of poets. They read to each other, but they mostly express innermost thoughts to themselves. The open poetry reading where everyone reads a poem, from the amateur to the well-published poet, I believe to be a great thing that should be done more. Everyone should express. . . . Poetry's pursuit has few monetary rewards. This activity, pursuit, becomes essential to the health of communities in a capitalist society where so much is geared toward accumulating money and the things it brings. . . . Poets are bridges to all communities of America. That potential should be developed. I think it is the unity of poets, poets of all stripes, in a real democratic way, irrespective of position, or social class, or publishing history; a unity of poets that could show a way in the near future that is upon us now. . . . "

DUBOSE HEYWARD (1885–1940), best known for his novel *Porgy* and the musical *Porgy and Bess* (written with the Gershwin brothers), published three volumes of poetry: *Carolina Chansons: Legends of the Low Country* (with Hervey Allen); *Skylines and Horizons*; and *Jasbo Brown and Selected Poems.*

EDWARD HIRSCH has published four books of poems: *For the Sleepwalkers; Wild Gratitude,* which won the National Book Critics Circle Award; *The Night Parade*; and *Earthly Measures.* He has received a Guggenheim Fellowship, a National Endowment for the Arts Creative Writing Fellowship, and the Rome Prize from the American Academy and Institute of Arts and Letters. He teaches at the University of Houston.

"Art Pepper (1925–1982) was probably the greatest alto saxophonist in the generation after Charlie Parker. He gives a searing portrait of himself as a junkie, a convict, and a musician in *Straight Life: The Story of Art Pepper* by Art and Laurie Pepper. My poem tries to give voice to his rage, to supply words for the harsh rhythms of his experience, and to mirror the structure of his solos, his furious timing and splintered lyricism, his nerve-shattering tones, the emotive way he improvised and blew *himself* into the night."

ANSELM HOLLO, poet and literary translator, is an associate professor in the M.F.A. writing and poetics program of the Naropa Institute in Boulder, Colorado. His most recent books are *Outlying Districts* and *Near Miss Haiku.*

"In the years immediately following my father's death (1967–1968), I had two vivid dreams in which he appeared, and these four lines are a literal transcription of one of them. The idea of a North European academic of fairly conservative tastes post-humously 'discovering' jazz struck me as both funny and poignant. During my London sojourn in the early sixties, I had DJ'ed a half-hour shortwave jazz program broadcast by the BBC's Finnish Service; in it, I presented an anthology of the great American art ranging from Sidney Bechet to Ornette Coleman (and was occasionally chided by my superiors for such eclecticism). I cannot imagine a world without jazz, be it hot or cool; it is one of the relatively few good reasons one has for enduring this century."

RICHARD HUGO (1923–1982) published many books of poems, including *The Lady in Kicking Horse Reservoir; What Thou Lovest Well Remains American;* and *The Collected Poems of Richard Hugo* (published posthumously). He was also the author of *The Triggering Town: Lectures and Essays on Poetry and Writing*, which includes this reflection:

"A man named Buzz Green worked with me years ago at the Boeing Company. He had once been a jazz musician and along with a man named Lu Waters had founded a jazz band well known in its day. Buzz once said of Lou McGarrity, a trombone player we both admired, 'He can play trombone with any symphony orchestra in the country but when he stands up to take a jazz solo he forgets everything he knows.' So if I seem to talk technique now and then and urge you to learn more, it is not so you will remember it when you write but so you can forget it. Once you have a certain amount of accumulated technique, you can forget it in the act of writing. Those moves that are naturally yours will stay with you and will come forth mysteriously when needed."

LYNDA HULL (1954–1994) published two books of poetry during her lifetime. *Ghost Money* received the 1986 Juniper Prize, the annual poetry award sponsored by the University of Massachusetts Press, and her second book of poems, *Star Ledger*, won the University of Iowa's Edwin Ford Piper Poetry Award. She received numerous honors and awards, including a Pushcart Prize, a fellowship from Yaddo, and an award from the National Endowment for the Arts. A third book, *The Only World,* was published posthumously.

T. R. HUMMER is the author of five books of poetry, including *The 18,000-Ton Olympic Dream* and *Walt Whitman in Hell.* His awards include a Guggenheim Fellowship in poetry, and he currently directs the program in creative writing at the University of Oregon.

ANGELA JACKSON has published several books of poetry, including *Voo Doo/Love Magic; Solo in the Boxcar Third Floor E; The Greenville Club; The Man with the White Liver;* and *Dark Legs and Silk Kisses.* She has received a number of awards and honors, including a Pushcart Prize for Poetry and the Chicago Sun Times/Friends of Literature Book of the Year for Poetry, and she is a four-time winner of the Illinois Arts Council Fiction Prize.

"When I was nineteen I sat on my dorm room bed listening to Billie Holiday's 'Golden Years' album and reading the liner notes. How excited I became when I learned she had made the aesthetic-technical decision to do with her voice what Prez did with his horn. One note at a time. I decided then I would do as she had done and make each *word* a note. Colored, shaded, nuanced, precised, innovated. Word for word. And Silences. Recently, at the National Black Arts Festival in Atlanta, after my reading, critic Clyde Taylor remarked to me that I (in my reading) reminded him of Billie Holiday. I hope that Lady smiled. I sure did."

RICHARD JACKSON is the author of three books of poetry, most recently *Alive All Day*. He is also the author of two books of criticism, an anthology of Slovene poetry, and the editor of *Poetry Miscellany, Mala Revija*, and the *PM* East European chapbook series. He teaches at the University of Tennessee–Chattanooga, where he has won several teaching awards and directs the Meacham Writers' Conference. He is a member of the Sarajevo Committee of the Slovene P.E.N., and his poems have been translated into several languages.

"Poetry is a means of transport, a metaphor, as the Roman critic Longinus once wrote, and as the root meaning of the word metaphor goes. It takes us to the unexpected, the unexplored, and discovers something new, and it does so, at least in American poetry, naturally in a form influenced by jazz: improvisation within a larger visionary or emotional structure or frame. It tends to take us very far out, just to the point where we think we can't come back—and then it takes us back, or rather, lets us see how it was all wrapped up or implied in the beginning. It is a wandering around in the imagination that is discovered to be a quest after all.

"'Shadows' attempts to suggest the sense of improvisation—the Italian *improvisatori* that Byron so admired would switch forms with moods. In a sense they were jazz poets. And so this poem tries to make its discoveries by trying to shift forms. It begins as a mirror sonnet, moves in its second paragraph to a sestina, then uses quatrains, a hybrid pantoum, rhymed couplets, and ends with the format of an English ode. Why? I guess the sense of surprise within these forms. The sestina and the hybrid pantoum approximate, for me, the movement of jazz and the *improvisatori* more than the others, yet there is a way in which they all keep searching for a form, something to contain the troubles they keep discovering, something to keep the addressee from taking her own life. I had been listening a lot to Charlie Parker at the time, and reading about his life, and I felt that this progression of forms said something about the music and life, too, used them as metaphors to take the poem into a dimension beyond its own personal concerns.

"But all this is done rather subconsciously for the most part. The discovery comes later. At the end of *Speak, Memory*, Nabokov describes how, waiting to depart for America, he could see, among the roofs of the city, behind a clothesline, the huge smokestack of the ship that would take him, 'as something in a scrambled picture— Find What the Sailor Has Hidden—that the finder cannot unsee once it has been seen.' Poetry gives us this new vision we cannot unsee: it is the boat, ready to transport us anywhere, ready to make sudden shifts and turns along the way where the little rifts of discovery are made."

DAVID JAUSS is the author of *Improvising Rivers*, a collection of poems, and co-editor, with Philip Dacey, of *Strong Measures*, an anthology of contemporary American poetry. Among his awards is a fellowship from the National Endowment for the Arts. A founding member of the Arkansas Jazz and Heritage Foundation, he teaches at the University of Arkansas at Little Rock.

"The two poems printed here are from a group of poems about jazz musicians—from James P. Johnson to Ornette Coleman—included in my book *Improvising Rivers*. Just as a jazz musician will 'open up' a melody to find everything that's in it, I tried, as a poet, to open up a moment in the lives of these musicians. While the poems imitate the procedure of jazz in this minor and oblique way, they are more concerned with exploring the lives behind the music than with describing the music itself. Their biological impulse stems, I think, from the fact that jazz is such a personal art form (Louis Armstrong equated it with the self, saying 'Jazz is only what you are') that those who love it, as I do, almost inevitably become interested in the people who created it. Also, since jazz is, as Philip Larkin said, 'the closest description of the unconscious we have,' it resists description by words—'the children of reason,' in Bill Evans's phrase—even more than other forms of music. But if language can't do full justice to jazz, it can nevertheless bring us closer to the musicians who created it and, by extension, to the music itself. I hope my poems accomplish this goal—and send the reader back to the beautiful, life-sustaining music created by their subjects."

LANCE JEFFERS (1919–1985) published several books of poetry, including *My Blackness Is the Beauty of This Land, When I Know the Power of My Black Hand*, and *O Africa, Where I Baked My Bread*. His last book was a novel titled *Witherspoon*.

JUNE JORDAN is the author of several books of poetry, including *Naming Our Destiny: New and Selected Poems*. She has also written plays and books of essays. Her awards include a Rockefeller grant, the American Academy in Rome Environmental Design Prize, and a National Endowment for the Arts Fellowship.

"Writing any kind of jazz poetry means that you try to exploit the musical possibilities of every syllable in relationship to every other syllable—for rhythm, for tempo (speeding up or slowing the reader/listener down) and for qualities of euphony or dissonance. In short, you work each part of each word as you would choose and then work a note in the context of a chord/a bar of music/an extended solo—improvised or not, etcetera. Clearly, then, you begin and you finish your revisions by reading the poem aloud: the *heard* qualities become far and away the most important factors determining the poem's failure or success."

ALLISON JOSEPH was born in London to parents of Caribbean heritage and raised in both Toronto and the Bronx. She is the author of *What Keeps Us Here*, which won the Ampersand Press Women Poetry Series competition and the John C. Zacharis Award from *Ploughshares*. She currently teaches at Southern Illinois University at Carbondale.

"The poem 'My Father's Heroes' stems from my dad's stubborn belief that blacks are superior. As proof, he played plenty of jazz for me, constantly reminded me of the superiority of black athletes (the Negro League players were some of his favorites, though he never saw them play), and made sure I knew the musicians who sometimes appeared on TV—like Cab Calloway or Lionel Hampton. It's ironic that he felt this way, that he so fervently embraced elements of this music and culture, since my father is of Caribbean descent. It isn't exactly a culture that's directly his. But his faith in it, his embrace of it, made an indelible mark on me. The poem was spurred by remembering all my father's proclamations of black superiority. Only a few white creative artists were allowed in my father's pantheon—Piaf being one of them. Piaf was not a jazz singer, of course, but it feels right to me that the poem ends up honoring her."

ROBERT KELLY has published more than fifty books of poetry, including *Under Words, Thor's Thrush*, and *Oahu*. He has also published a number of plays, novels, and books of short stories.

KEORAPETSE KGOSITSILE, a South African poet, has been living in exile since 1961. He has published several books of poetry, including *My Name Is Afrika, The Present Is a Dangerous Place to Live*, and *When the Clouds Clear*. He has also edited a book of contemporary poetry from Africa titled *The Word Is Here*. His awards and honors include the Conrad Kent Rivers Memorial Poetry Award and the Harlem Cultural Council Poetry Award.

YUSEF KOMUNYAKAA has published five books of poetry: *Copacetic, I Apologize for the Eyes in My Head* (which won the San Francisco Book Center Award), *Dien Cai Dau, Magic City*, and *Neon Vernacular* (which won the Kingsley Tufts Award and the Pulitzer Prize). He currently teaches at Indiana University.

OLIVER LaGRONE is the author of *Footfalls, They Speak of Dawns*, and *Dawnfire and Other Poems*. He is primarily known, however, as a visual artist. He studied sculpture under Carl Miles, having "decided to become a sculptor," he writes, "at age four" (1910). He has had many one-man shows and is currently working on a sculpture of Rosa Parks.

VACHEL LINDSAY (1879–1931) published many books of poetry during his lifetime, including *The Congo and Other Poems, The Daniel Jazz and Other Poems, Going-to-the-Stars*, and *Collected Poems*. A three-volume set of his poetry and prose appeared posthumously and includes this statement:

"[J]azz is hectic, has the leer of the bad-lands in it, and first, last and always is hysteric. It is full of the dust of the dirty dance. The Saxophone, its chief instrument[,] is the most diseased instrument in all modern music."

DOUGHTRY "DOC" LONG was born in Atlanta, Georgia, and grew up in Trenton, New Jersey. He has lived and worked in Africa and the Caribbean. He was a member of the John Killens Writers Workshop in New York City and is presently a teacher in the Trenton Public School System.

"Jazz poetry comes close to being an emotional/cognitive and verbal improvisation played to a local insight."

MICHAEL LONGLEY is the author of many books of poetry, including *Gorse Fires,* which won the Whitbread Prize for Poetry, and *Selected Poems 1963–1980*. He has also edited two books about the arts from Ulster, as well as Louis MacNeice's *Selected Poems*. He has written many scripts for the BBC's educational programs and has been the subject of numerous television films.

"I've always enjoyed jazz, but I took to it in a big way the year I got married. That the suffering and degradation of slavery should bring forth so much redemptive energy and beauty remains for me miraculous and almost unendurably moving. At another level I love the way artists such as Fats Waller and Louis Armstrong make difficult maneuvers look effortless (unlike so many pop musicians: too much rock 'n' roll, for instance, takes from jazz the insistent rhythm and leaves the poetry behind). It's important for a formalist like me to be reminded of the power of improvisation. The spontaneity of jazz must be one of the best antidotes against authoritarianism, totalitarianism, against systems that would tell us what to think and feel. Its emergence in the century of the jackboot is of the greatest cultural importance. Jazz is arguably the twentieth century's most significant contribution to the culture of the world. The Nazis hated it. They were frightened of swing. Syncopation is the opposite of the goose-step. 'The natural noise of good'—to quote Philip Larkin. Heaven will be full of saxophones and trumpets for those who can play, and kazoos for the rest of us. The joint will be jumping!"

THOMAS LUX teaches at Sarah Lawrence College. He has published several books of poetry, most recently *Split Horizon,* which received the Kingsley Tufts Award.

NAOMI LONG MADGETT published her first book, *Songs to a Phantom Nightingale,* in 1941 and has subsequently published seven volumes of poetry, most recently *Exits and Entrances*, the award-winning *Octavia and Other Poems,* and *Remembrances of Spring: Collected Early Poems.* Her poems have appeared in more than 125 anthologies here and abroad. Madgett is also editor of two anthologies, including the highly acclaimed *Adam of Ifé: Black Women in Praise of Black Men,* for which she also wrote the foreword. Recent honors include the Michigan Artist Award (Governor's Arts Award) and an honorary Doctor of Fine Arts from Michigan State University. She is professor emerita of English at Eastern Michigan University.

"As a poet I am not inclined to follow trends or appeal to whatever audience seems to be most receptive at the moment. I write out of my own black experience (real, vicarious, imagined), as the mood strikes me, and I believe that, if I am honest, readers will eventually discover and identify with my work. Black music has been a vital part of my experience, especially spirituals, blues, and the more melodic and lyrical forms of jazz."

HAKI MADHUBUTI has been the editor and publisher of Third World Press since 1967. He is the author of many books of poetry (some published under the name Don L. Lee), including *Don't Cry, Scream; Earthquakes and Sunrise Missions;* and *Killing Memory, Seeking Ancestors.* He has received a fellowship from the National Endowment for the Arts as well as other awards and honors.

RICK MADIGAN's poems have appeared in *Poetry, Ploughshares,* the *North American Review, Crazyhorse,* and elsewhere. He currently teaches at East Stroudsburg University.

"When you're listening to Booker Little play 'We Speak,' it's a bitter thing to realize that you're hearing a man with one year, more or less to live, who'll die at twenty-three years old, just coming into his full powers. What might he have played had he lived a little longer? Our notions of how early excellence develops in those who are gone too soon may have more to do with our dismay and disappointment, the brittle chill we feel in our comfortable bones, than with how anyone could become so good so fast. The only consolation's in the music Little left us, different now, precious, because of what won't follow.

"Of course, there's a small consolation in hearing his influence on many of the young trumpet players, who clearly have listened to their predecessors. And, in addition, some of the legendary figures are still around, including one of my favorite trombonists, Curtis Fuller."

WILLIAM MATTHEWS has published ten books of poetry, including *Selected Poems and Translations 1969–1991*. He has also published a book of essays titled *Curiosities*. He currently teaches at City College in New York. In a recent interview for the *Georgia Review* (with Yusef Komunyakaa and moderated by Robert Kelly), Matthews had this to say about poetry and jazz:

"If the ultimate sources for poetry and jazz are the life of the emotions, the extreme difficulty of describing that life, and the great spiritual cost of *not* trying to describe it, then poetry and jazz are rooted at the very center of what it's like to be human. They ought to be of wide interest, therefore, and yet both poetry and jazz find themselves existing in tenuous relation to a comparatively small audience. Their vitality is honored in largely sanctuarial settings—colleges, art institutes, community centers, and so on. Outside the sanctuaries, the situation reminds me of Yogi Berra's comment about baseball fans not coming out to the stadium: 'If they want to stay away in droves, you can't stop them.'

"The contrast between the centrality of the enterprise and the size of the audience is not something we should necessarily feel guilty about, as if we had ourselves caused it. But there is a danger that despite deep and powerful emotional bases, poetry and jazz can turn into museum arts, losing the nourishment that more direct access to an audience can provide. We couldn't—and shouldn't—have asked John Coltrane to back off and play a lot of four-four stuff in order to enlarge his audience. The artist's job is not to solve the problem—but the problem exists."

KENNETH MAY, a member of Etheridge Knight's last Free Peoples' Poetry Workshop, is the author of a poetry chapbook, *Somewhere Down Low*. Currently, he lives in the Washington D.C. area, where he co-directs (with Mark Williams) a program which supports male students through their high school years.

"I come from a city with a rich jazz history—Indianapolis, Indiana. Freddie Hubbard, Wes Montgomery, J. J. Johnson, Slide Hampton, and Dave Baker are some of the musicians who began their careers down on old Indiana Avenue in clubs that were torn down before my birth. I didn't listen to jazz while growing up. As close as jazz came to entering our house were the Chicago and Al Green records my father and mother listened to while doing laundry. Outside the home, though, I often came into contact with jazz but, like people who recognize each other and never say hello, we just nodded and continued down the road. But I had a friend, Mike Niederpruem, who loved jazz and played trumpet in all the school bands. Miles Davis was his favorite musician. Jazz first touched my ears at his house. I wish I could say I was a hip enough twelve-year-old kid to get it, but I wasn't—and didn't. More than a decade later—by the way of the blues—I finally listened to the voice inside my head and bought my first jazz albums: Miles's *Kind of Blue,* Coltrane's *Giant Steps,* Bird's *Savoy Sessions Vol. 1,* and Billie Holiday's *Lady Sings the Blues.* At the same time, I began to recognize and approach poetry as a kind of shelter and vehicle for self-expression. The poem 'Valentine's Day' comes out of those first few nights when jazz and poetry made their introduction."

MICHAEL MCCLURE is a poet, playwright, and novelist. He performs his poetry with the Doors keyboardist Ray Manzarek. The first CD of their work, *Love Lion,* has been released and the second album, *Haikus and Peyote Poem,* is in preparation. In 1994 they performed in the Lollapalooza Festival and at Town Hall in Manhattan. Recently McClure performed the poem "For Monk" with bassist Rob Wasserman at a celebration in honor of William Burroughs and Hal Wilner. The poem was originally published, with other jazz poems, in *The New Book/A Book of Torture* in 1961. The poet also reads "For Monk" without musical accompaniment on the *Jazz Speak* album. McClure's recent work includes two books of poetry (*Rebel Lions* and *Simple Eyes*), a book of essays (*Scratching the Beat Surface*), and selected interviews (*Lighting the Corners*).

"My poetry would not be what it is if I had not heard Thelonious Monk when I was seventeen years old—and Monk would not have meant what he meant if I had not been reading William Blake. I was prepared, in part, for Blake by seeing Jackson Pollock's work. After I heard Monk I began listening to the old Blue Note albums as they appeared. Bud Powell, Shadow Wilson, Kenny Clarke all came gyring out the grooves of 33 and 1/3rd albums and became deepening parts of my life. I was a kid running around with hipsters and beboppers between Kansas City and Wichita and at the same time I was reading the mystical works of Jacob Böhme. Jack Kerouac called this all a 'Mersion of Missy,' and he's right. It's all in my out-of-print autobiographical novel, *The Mad Cub.*"

THOMAS MCGRATH (1916–1990) published more than twenty books of poetry in his lifetime, including *Selected Poems 1938–1988.* He also published two novels. His many awards include a National Endowment for the Arts Fellowship, a Guggenheim Fellowship, and the Lenore Marshall-Nation Prize.

JAMES MCKEAN is the author of *Headlong,* which won the 1987 Great Lakes Colleges Association's New Writer Award for poetry, and *Tree of Heaven,* which won the Iowa Poetry Prize. His poems have appeared in magazines such as *Atlantic, Kenyon Review, Poetry,* and *Poetry Northwest.* He lives in Iowa City.

"I agree with Hayden Carruth's explanation that jazz is spontaneous improvisation within a fixed and simple form, something that he admits himself is common knowledge. Of course, this thinking can apply to the writing and reading of poetry—the voice in the poem working against the expectations of form, the words and rhythms at odds with the given and then the wonderful reward of surprise, a new tune played out on an old expectation, 'lyric inventiveness,' 'a clear line,' 'spontaneous, personal,' and 'on-the-spot invention.' What's interesting here is that this quoted language is from an Otis Ferguson article, 'Young Man with a Horn,' written in 1936, describing Bix Beiderbecke's music and Jack Teagarden's 'beautiful eight bar creation' in a recording Hoagy Carmichael made of his own 'Georgia.'

"Thus it is for poetry too—that form is absolutely necessary, either given by tradition or discovered organically in the first few lines, so that the clear, new voice can explore, revise, spin, and renew. At some point, the set figure is let go, memorized, and then reinvented enthusiastically. The swirl and speed of Coltrane, for example. The lines of Duncan or Hughes. In his *Autobiography,* Mark Twain suggests that the older he got the easier it was to remember things that never really happened. Yes, it's the blue vaults he improvised between primary feathers on the summer day he remembered lying back and watching a hawk soar. It's Kerouac's 'it.' And the result is an immediate tension, a kind of wonderful burning and attention on the instant, on the notes or words neither abstracted nor conceptual but *played*."

SANDRA MCPHERSON is the author of fourteen books, most recently *The God of Interdeterminacy.* Her many awards include two Ingram Merrill grants, three National Endowment for the Arts Fellowships, and a Guggenheim Fellowship. She currently teaches at the University of California at Davis.

"Writing these poems was for me a way of attentive listening to a great bluesman's art. Once the poems completed themselves, they became documentation of specific performances. Blues magazines are good at interviewing blues artists to find out who played with whom on which old recording, but I found interviews frustratingly silent on the mysteries of voice and instrumental sound and underlying feeling and well-thought-out framing—the smarts, the subtle and surprising expressive detailing—of blues that shape the magic. These poems try to see what Junior's harp, body, singing voice, and offstage talk demonstrate about those aspects of his art. 'Spider' derives from viewing a 1982 videotape; 'Suspension' and 'Metaphysics' from attending two performances in the late 1980s, with Buddy Guy, Junior's co-star, at The Palms in Davis, California. I am thankful to my partner, Walter, for getting me backstage."

DAVID MELTZER is the author of many books of poetry, including *Tens* (edited with Kenneth Rexroth), *Yesod, Six, Harps, The Name,* and *Arrows: Selected Poetry, 1957–1992.* He has edited various thematic anthologies including *The San Francisco Poets: Interviews; The Secret Garden: Classical Kabbalistic Texts; Birth: Texts, Songs, Prayers, and Stories*; and *Reading Jazz. Orf,* one of ten erotic novels he wrote in the '60s, has been reprinted recently, as has *The Agency* trilogy. Vanguard Records reissued his late '60s rock band's first album, *Serpent Power,* on CD. He is currently working on a biographical and cultural study of the influential Los Angeles artist Wallace Berman. With poet Clark Coolidge, vocalist/songwriter Tina Meltzer, and assorted musicians, poets, and artists, he is part of MIX, a performance ensemble. Meltzer currently teaches in the undergraduate humanities program and the graduate poetics program at New College of California in San Francisco.

"Jazz as event, practice, language, culture, has been a central influence on (and in) my work since I first heard bebop in 1947 when I was ten years old. Despite an ongoing accumulation of history, memory, vocabularies, I remain grounded in the radical ethos of the hipster. An insubordinate culture of everyday mysteries transformed by enormous gifts of improvisation."

ADRIAN MITCHELL has published more than ten books of poetry, including *For Beauty Douglas: Collected Poems 1953–1979*. He has also published over thirty-five plays, as well as screenplays, radio plays, television plays, novels, and children's books. In addition, he has edited two anthologies of poetry.

> "Most people ignore most poetry
>   because
>   most poetry ignores most people."

ERNST MOERMAN (1897–1944), a Belgian poet and playwright, published three books of poetry: *Fantômas 33, Vie imaginaire de Jésus-Christ*, and *37°5*. He was also a member of Robert Goffin's "Doctor Mysterious Six" jazz band. His poem "Armstrong" first appeared in *Fantômas 33* (1933) and then, translated into English by Samuel Beckett, in Nancy Cunard's anthology *Negro* (1934).

AMUS MOR was featured in Woodie King's anthology *Black Spirits: A Festival of New Black Poets in America*. His work was also part of a sound recording with the same title. For King's anthology, Mor wrote that he had taught at the University of Massachusetts until he "decided that there was little possible relevant work that can be done inside the 'system.'" He appeared on Muhal Richard Abrams's *Levels and Degrees of Light* but has been very reclusive for most of his life.

LARRY NEAL (1937–1981) was a poet, playwright, and essayist, as well as the co-editor (with Amiri Baraka) of the anthology *Black Fire. Visions of a Liberated Future: Black Arts Movement Writings,* which features selections of his poetry, essays, and plays, appeared posthumously and includes this statement from his essay "The Ethos of the Blues":

> "The ethos of the blues, then, is the musical manifestation of one's individual cultural experiences in Afro-America with which members of the black community can identify. The blues performer has a talk with himself about the problem, analyzes the situation, and then takes his own advice to remedy it. He thereby opens up his soul to the world and allows it to see the sadness, the heartache, and the joys he has sustained in life—the trials and tribulations that get him down, but nevertheless, his determination to 'make it'—and if he can get a witness, someone who can testify to the same feelings and experiences, then he has succeeded in revealing the essential essence of human experiences."

MWATABU OKANTAH's books of poetry include *Afreeka Brass* and *Collage*. Currently he puts most of his energy into performing his poetry with the group The Mwatabu Okantah/Eric Gould Project.

> "When I first read the introduction to Stephen Henderson's *Understanding the New Black Poetry,* the initial impact was revelatory. It provided me with a culturally relevant definition of poetry that made sense to my ears. I did not *hear* in the alien sounds of English sonnets. I *did* hear in the cacophony of black life sounds that surrounded me.

Put another way, Henderson's seminal work allowed me to place contemporary black poetry within the context of traditional African modes of expression: drum, dance, and song. In African terms, the poet is storyteller. The poet is master of eloquence and keeper of the sacred lore of the folk. The poet is both healer and historian. The poets are 'the guardians of the soul of the nation.' From this perspective, the black tradition in poetry here in the USA is part of the larger, New World African tradition—a Pan-African tradition.

"Ultimately, I cannot separate my poetry from my personal struggle to develop and maintain a healthy, black identity. The act of writing became my primary means of self-expression and self-discovery. It was a graduate student, Sis. Odara, who introduced me to serious black music. She opened me up with the Crusaders' 'First Crusade.' She blew me away with 'A Love Supreme' by John Coltrane. She gave me copies of Wright's *Native Son* and *The Autobiography of Malcolm X* to read, and I have not been the same since.

"Black poets give voices to all those unfolding stories our people need to have told. For a long time, I did not know how to describe this thing I sensed growing inside of my being. I could either give in, and become one with it, or I could divide, fight it, and experience personal turmoil. Although I tried mightily, it was not in me to fight against this power. I moved toward the word sounds I heard whispering inside my inner ear. Ancestral voices. Afreekan voices. For the poets, it is not in us to fight against *being* black oneness. Tradition. My teachers helped me to understand there is no single poet who speaks for black people. Our strong voices together comprise an ensemble of one collective voice."

RON OVERTON has published three books of poetry, including *Hotel Me: Poems for Gil Evans*. His poetry and prose have appeared in numerous magazines and anthologies, including *Poetry Northwest, Commonweal, Massachusetts Review, American Poetry Review,* and *Downbeat*. He has received both a National Endowment for the Arts Fellowship in poetry and a New York State Foundation for the Arts Writing Fellowship.

"Jazz music has been a joyful obsession since junior high in the '50s. It took over so thoroughly it drove out any interest in then-evolving rock 'n' roll (Ringo who?), hence was a social liability in high school and even later. When I wore my 'Dizzy for President' button, they thought I meant Dizzy Dean.

"'Blues in "C"' is a response to the music (and passing) of Gil Evans, a close second to Ellington in finding what large jazz ensembles might include. Although he is best known for his orchestral settings for Miles Davis recordings in the '50s, fewer listeners are aware of the wilder, looser, more 'outside' compositions and recompositions of the '80s, when I believe Evans solved the problems of integrating electronic and acoustic instruments, pop (e.g., Hendrix) and jazz riffs, free playing and traditional forms. It's hair-raising stuff. What interested me into writing the poem was how Evans got more open and experimental as he aged—the opposite of what you might expect. The poem borrows its title and four-part structure from one of these later Evans songs. His Monday Night Orchestra (at Sweet Basil, in NYC) revived for me a waning interest in jazz and was like electroshock therapy for mid-life questions and various sorrows.

"Beyond such specifics, I find myself influenced by jazz in two ways. First, I think the best poetry is similarly improvisational, full of surprises for the writer as well as the reader, lyrical enough to carry you away, but defamiliarizing enough to bring you back, provoke you, keep it all from being just a nice warm cultural buzz. Writing poems, I have in mind a good song—that certain amount of expectation met in the 'head,' plenty of twists in the solo, enough chops so that technique doesn't get in the way, and a good ear for when to stop.

"Second, I'm lucky, I live near NYC and get to hear a lot of live jazz. I like hanging with jazz musicians. I like their lack of pretension, their practical solution to problems, their relaxed sense of self, their sense of humor, their intuitive intelligence, their friendliness. But especially, their lack of pretension. They're serious about art, of course, and play that way—so they don't have to posture as artists. And there's ego, obviously. But the jazz doesn't happen without being open and in some way empty of self—so the listening that's essential for collective improvisation can take place.

"I feel especially inspired by the kind of player who goes his or her own way, at the expense of being unnoticed by the jazz media and underrecorded by the record companies. I'm thinking of independent musicians like Gil Goldstein, John Clark, Chris Hunter, Marilyn Crispell, Kenwood Dennard, Maria Schneider, Dave Bargeron, Mike Mossman, Dave Taylor—players in mid-career, all doing original work, all admired by other musicians, but unknown to you if you have to depend on the record chains and jazz mags for what's happening.

"I have little interest in using poetry to imitate jazz or to be 'performed' with jazz. What's to gain? Words pale next to the heat of good jazz, which drives right to the bone. Billie Holiday? The poetry is in the voice, as instrument, not the words. Listen to early records, when she was given third-rate material: the jazz is in the singing, as it transcends the trite, corny language."

RAYMOND R. PATTERSON is the author of *Twenty-Six Ways of Looking at a Black Man and Other Poems, For K.L.,* and *Elemental Blues.* His awards and honors include a Borestone Mountain Award, a fellowship from the National Endowment for the Arts, and a Creative Artists Public Service grant.

"The challenge of the blues to American poetry receives little attention. Huddled on the mental coasts of this continent, their backs to the wild heartland beyond their crude stockades, still-colonial poets yearn outward toward forms and an aesthetic to manifest the native spirit (or boisterously deny the need for any) cavalierly dismissing the home-grown product, the blues. Poor Walt, born too soon. The blues would have kept his feet to the ground. (But wherefore Melville?) Poor Emily. The blues would have set her free. What excuse have we? Thoreau wrote: 'I went to the woods because I wished to live deliberately, to front only the essential facts of life, and see if I could not learn what it had to teach.' For that reason I went to the blues."

USENI EUGENE PERKINS is the author of several books of poetry, including *Black Is Beautiful, Silhouette,* and *Midnight Blues in the Afternoon and Other Poems.* For the last thirty years, he has spent much of his time as a sociologist, helping in particular disadvantaged youths.

"There is a strong confluence between jazz and poetry; both are lyrical and rhythmic and enjoy a sense of improvisation. For these reasons, and many more, I have attempted to infuse in my poetry some of the qualities that are intrinsic to jazz. In a generic sense, I believe the poet is fundamentally a vocal instrumentalist who experiments with new forms and writes as though he is composing a musical score for a combo or orchestra.

"These poems are an expression of my musical intuition and celebration of some of the jazz icons that have inspired me."

DUDLEY RANDALL is the founding publisher of Broadside Press, one of the most important presses in the history of jazz poetry. His books of poetry include *Ballad of Birmingham, More to Remember: Poems of Four Decades,* and *A Litany of Friends: Poems Selected and New.* He has also edited four anthologies.

EUGENE B. REDMOND was named Poet Laureate of East St. Louis, Illinois, in 1976, the year he published *Drumvoices: The Mission of Afro-American Poetry.* At Southern Illinois University in Edwardsville, where he is Professor of English and chairman of the creative writing program, Redmond has revived the name *Drumvoices [Revue]* for his new journal of literary, cultural, and visual arts. During more than twenty-five years of writing, cultural work, and teaching, he has also served as literary executor of the estate of Henry Dumas. He edited six collections of Dumas's works for posthumous publication, including *Goodbye, Sweetwater* and *Knees of a Natural Man.* Among Redmond's own volumes of poetry—which have garnered him such prizes as an American Book Award, a National Endowment for the Arts Creative Writing Fellowship, a Pushcart Prize, and an Illinois Author-of-the-Year citation—are *The Eye in the Ceiling.* He is currently writing an epic poem inspired by the life of prima ballerina Katherine Dunham, his mentor and longtime friend.

"Birthtonics, deathbones, transformations and travesties. One journeyman said the blues 'ain't nothing but a botheration on your mind.' Another, a literary-cultural pioneer, called the blues an autobiographical chronicle evoked by personal catastrophe. A journeywoman of nasty elegance got the blues from strange fruit on southern trees. I can get to botheration, catastrophe and strange fruit, hookups that jibe with the cultural cum blues matrix of my yawning years, and with my journeyman ministry as a blues poet or bluesician. So-called blues tone, with their accompanying wails, rails and takes of what ails, were fermented in the ritual bowels of Africa. Griots, midwives and exhorters, who played gourds and drums, were ripped from African matrix, replanted in the black diaspora, and due to botherations on their minds, intoned the blues or autobiographical chronicles. Aesthetics of pain, aesthetics of orgasm, aesthetics of heavy weather, aesthetics of sweet hurt. Blues got handed down from moans, shouts, lash-induced screams, spirituals, human spillage, field hollers and gone-wrong love. Blues then mated with Eurocentric sounds and delivered jazz. Recoupling with spirituals, blues gave us gospel. Today, blues inform and form rap."

DAVID RIVARD is the author of *Torque,* which won the 1987 Agnes Lynch Starrett Poetry Prize. Among his awards are two fellowships from the National Endowment for the Arts, fellowships from the Massachusetts Arts Foundation and the Fine Arts

Work Center in Provincetown, and a Pushcart Prize. His poems and essays have appeared in *Poetry, Ploughshares, North American Review, TriQuarterly,* and other magazines. A contributing editor at the *Harvard Review,* he teaches at Tufts University and in the M.F.A. writing program at Vermont College.

"If my poems are influenced at all by jazz—and I think they are—it's in ways that are multiple but subtle. Improvisation in the act of composing for one thing, because the evolving and unraveling of the tune is a thing I have always loved—play and shape, the random winging away and back, refrains, lyric poolings, running a buzz saw through the song and coming back with the melody, fresh. Also, my sense of the line, which wants to convey intonations, shifts in register, clashes of diction and character— some of the way this gets marked off by punctuation and white space is similar to the way some players use silence. There's a comma placement in a Frank O'Hara poem that reminds me of Miles. And why not? As for 'Baby Vallejo,' well, in Provincetown I did live in the same building as Myron Stout—a gentle, erudite soul who had gone blind but once had been one of the best of the Abstract Expressionist painters—though, actually, we never listened to Dolphy together. But I like to think of this part of the poem as a kind of wish fulfillment—as it could have happened. So. Stout, Dolphy, and dear Vallejo. What else is poetry for except to save people? Which is another thing it has in common with jazz."

CONRAD KENT RIVERS (1933–1968) published three books of poetry during his lifetime: *Perchance to Dream, Othello; These Black Bodies and This Sunburnt Face;* and *Dusk at Selma.* Two other books appeared posthumously: *The Still Voice of Harlem* and *The Wright Poems.*

JEREMY ROBSON's books of poetry include *Poems for Jazz, Thirty-Three Poems, In Focus,* and *Travelling.* He has edited collections, such as *Poems from Poetry and Jazz in Concert,* and has made jazz poetry recordings.

CAROLYN M. RODGERS is the author of several books of poetry, including *Paper Soul, How I Got Ovah: New and Selected Poems,* and *Morning Glory.* She has also published a novel, *A Little Lower Than Angels.* Her awards include the Conrad Kent Rivers Award, a fellowship from the National Endowment for the Arts, and the Gwendolyn Brooks Fellowship.

"I was born in the ghetto in Chicago, Illinois, during the forties. I grew up near the infamous 47th Street. There were nightclubs all along the way and all the famous blues singers came through at one time or another to the 708 Club.

"I walked through my childhood, like a sponge, soaking up the soul sounds of artists like Sam Cooke, Nat 'King' Cole, Muddy Waters, and Mavis Staples and the Staple Singers, and many many more. I was rocked by the music and poetry of radio ministers from every imaginable denomination, and by my mother's love for the poetry of Paul Laurence Dunbar.

"I began to write poetry and songs when I was in the third grade. I wrote exclusively about trees, stars, birds, anything that had to do with nature. I never dreamed or even thought about becoming a writer. What was that? I was merely doing something to pass the time. Straight through high school and college, I wrote, never giving any of it serious thought. I was just spewing gut by that time. I was not ever giving back any of the soul music or poetry that was in me from my youth.

"Then I became acquainted with people like Gwendolyn Brooks, Margaret Walker, and Hoyt Fuller. It was during the 1960s and I became part of a group known as OBAC (Oh-bah-see) Writers' Workshop. At that time I learned about a black aesthetic in literature and in the arts in general. I was taught artistic responsibility and accountability to the black community. My way of being and seeing, thinking and writing changed, of course.

"I acquired purpose and vision which were new, and a racial perspective and consciousness. Now I work at developing a poetry that is as broadly human as it is specifically racial. I strive to write a poetry of conscience and heart that at least sometimes, if not always, transcends ethnic boundaries."

MURIEL RUKEYSER (1913–1980) published eighteen books of poetry during her lifetime, including *The Collected Poems of Muriel Rukeyser*. Since her death, two important collections have been published: *Out of Silence: Selected Poems* and *The Muriel Rukeyser Reader*.

SADIQ grew up right around the corner from Hitsville U.S.A. in the neighborhood where Detroit caught fire and changed the course of American history. He has been published in many quarterlies and anthologies, and recently he collaborated with clarinetist Don Byron on an album of Byron's music for which he penned and recited the title piece "Tuskegee Experiment." As a percussionist, he has performed and/or recorded with the Fifth Dimension, Eartha Kitt, Dance Theater of Harlem, Geri Allen, Brandon Ross, and Sonny Fortune, to name a few. He has also completed a manuscript paying homage to the painter Wifredo Lam.

"I find myself staring at the blank screen (read page) listening to the groan of all that I have learned. I press the buttons that say 'Poem' and 'Jazz' and, depending on my condition, a composition gradually appears. When the hypnosis wears off, I click 'Print.'"

NTOZAKE SHANGE, a prolific poet, playwright, and novelist, has published many books. Recent books of poetry include *From Okra to Greens, Nappy Edges,* and *I Live in Music*. She regularly performs her poetry with live jazz accompaniment.

CHARLES SIMIC is the author of more than twenty books of poems, including *The World Doesn't End, The Book of Gods and Devils,* and *Selected Poems 1963–1983*. He has edited and translated several books and has received many awards and honors, including the Pulitzer Prize for Poetry and fellowships from the National Endowment for the Arts, the Guggenheim Foundation, the Ingram Merrill Foundation, and the MacArthur Foundation.

"Between the years 1958 and 1970, at least two to three times per week, I could be found in some jazz club in New York City tapping my foot and nursing a beer. I once stopped Mr. Monk and told him how much I loved his playing. The great man looked past me in the direction of the bathroom and went off without even a nod of acknowledgment. Still, these were the happiest times in my life."

RALPH SNEEDEN has published his poetry and fiction in *New England Review, Gray's Sporting Journal, Sycamore Review, New Virginia Review, Whetstone, Hayden's Ferry Review,* and other magazines. With his wife and two children, he recently moved from the Boston area to Illinois, where he is the English Department Chair at Lake Forest Academy, just north of Chicago. "The first jazz LP I bought," he notes, "was Buster Williams's *Heartbeat,* after hearing him and Kenny Barron in a free concert in a UMass dining hall, spring of 1979."

"I suppose 'Coltrane and My Father' suggests that jazz has entered my poetry more metaphorically than musically. But beyond the individual legends, the stories of its musicians' lives, the persistence of this music to test the structures which surround it comes closer to refining my understanding of life and art than anything else. As trite as it may seem, the standard 'changes' are set before us, especially when we start our own families. The patterns are inescapable. We move through them, some of us more loosely, less obediently than others. Sometimes the departures work, sometimes they don't. It all comes down to how we (aspiring maverick soloists) balance these flights—what we *want* to do, with what is *expected* of us. In the waves of repetition and rhythm surrounding us and sustaining us, how do we avoid doing the same thing over and over again? Miles Davis, when asked to play 'Stella by Starlight' after beginning his forays into amplified fusion, said, 'If I had to play that shit again, I'd have a heart attack.'"

A. B. SPELLMAN has published numerous books and articles on the arts, including *Art Tatum: A Critical Biography* and *Four Lives in the Bebop Business,* as well as one collection of poetry titled *The Beautiful Days.* From 1978 to 1993, he was director of the National Endowment for the Arts' expansion arts program. More recently, he was named associate deputy for program coordination. Prior to joining the endowment, he was an artist-in-residence at Morehouse College; taught varied courses in African American culture; offered courses in modern poetry, creative writing, and jazz at Emory, Rutgers, and Harvard universities; and was a television and radio commentator.

"I always have envied painters because they can work with the music turned up loud while I cannot write a word with Charlie Parker on. All of the painters who are friends of mine dance as they work. They stroke in time and review their progress with tunes in their heads. Their work is action, music is action, action in sound integrates with action in color. And so they talk about their work as if they were John Coltrane. They describe blocks of color as chords, strokes as musical lines, tones are minor and major keys replete with blue notes, patterns as rhythms. I cannot do this.

"I have had periods in which I have started my work from a place so far from reason that only the maddest of surrealists live there. But that is different from the continual rearrangement of the synapses that Cecil Taylor accomplishes so easily. Words make me tune my senses on reality and reason. Somewhere I have written of myself that, 'like all black dancers, I am played by drums and saxophones,' but I have never been able to achieve in poetry the immediate staccato caress of bebop. The sound and colors that I can call to the poem may at best have a kind of swing but they are not swing.

"So I cannot claim to be a jazz poet. Though rhythm and sound are important to my work, I am more a poet of the eye than of the ear; more a poet of the page than of the stage. My work is neither oral nor aural.

"God, I envy painters."

LORENZO THOMAS is the author of *Chances Are Few* and *The Bathers.* His work has appeared in many anthologies and has been broadcast on radio. He currently teaches English at the University of Houston–Downtown.

"Because it is conceived as a tonal evocation of the spirit of Charles Parker (1920–1955), 'Historiography' is a poem designed for oral recitation. It is a solo constructed in the bop saxophone style. The poem was written to be performed with a jazz orchestra of three to seven pieces, using traditional 1940s bebop instrumentation. In its own way, the poem is an investigation of the sonic developments pioneered by Parker and his associates.

"'Historiography' has been performed in New York City sittin' in with the Wes Belcamp group at the Village Door (1972) and with the Ric Murray Trio on a poetry and jazz program entitled *UNION* at Sir James' Pub (April 18, 1974). The piece has also been performed with Lanny Steele and the Texas Southern University Jazz Ensemble at the Westheimer Art Fair in Houston, Texas (September 1974)."

ASKIA MUHAMMAD TOURÉ is the author of *JuJu, Songhai,* and *Samory Touré,* a political biography of the nineteenth-century Mandinka anticolonial freedom-fighter, which he co-authored with artist Tom Feelings. He served as an editor of two of the leading journals in the 1960s and 1970s, *Black Dialogue* and the *Journal of Black Poetry.* He received an American Book Award for Literature for his epic "novel-in-verse," *From the Pyramids to the Projects.* Currently, he is completing *Dawn Song!,* a volume of epic poems, and *Bronze Odysseys,* a volume of essays, narratives, inspirational meditations, and poems. He lives and writes in Atlanta and is co-founder of a poetry reading series, *Klub Kuumba.* He also performs with a jazz musical ensemble called *Song of Life,* which interprets his poetry, along with that of Larry Neal and others.

"My current work has focused upon the resurrection and restoration of the ancient archetypes of African heritage peoples and humanity. It began with earlier books and has gained depth and momentum with my current work-in-progress, a volume of narratives and verse, entitled *The Osirian Rhapsody.* It is a combination of historical restoration and the poetic imagination. In the process, I return the reader to what modern science has declared as the origins of humanity, with the early hominids and neolithic peoples in the Great Lakes region of Southeast Africa. Utilizing a combination of epic and lyrical verse, lined with prose narrative, I attempt to re-create and explore key aspects of the ancient, primordial world, leading to the establishment of Nile Valley Civilization (ancient Nubia and Pharaonic Egypt). I then explore the Egyptian archetypes (Isis, Osiris, Thoth, Hathor, etc.), linking them with Egyptian rulers and peoples. I also attempt, in the process, to show their presence and relevance to the lives and destinies of modern Africans and African heritage peoples.

"My aesthetic development as a literary artist is based upon the powerful folk culture of African Americans, particularly black music. I have attempted to link the lyrical intensity of 'jazz' and blues to the visionary, prophetic tradition. As such, it is an effort to resurrect the communal voice of the griot (oral historian), the black orator/preacher and social visionary, with direct roots in the African oral tradition. My work is composed of vivid imagery, lyricism, a multitude of voices, and a multitude of experimental forms in the modernist tradition. Additionally, I am deeply influenced by the translated work of the Chilean Nobel Laureate Pablo Neruda, particularly the 'Canto General,' and 'The Heights of Macchu Picchu,' his epic efforts to define South American Man/Woman, along with the brilliant Romanticism of William Butler Yeats in restoring the ancient Irish myths, legends, and cultural traditions to his struggling people. Those two bards have been my literary mentors and role models.

"In my early (1969) epic poem, 'JuJu,' I attempted to achieve for Afrikan American visionary verse what major poets Dante, in renaissance Italy, and Iqbal, in modern India, had accomplished. Dante was led by Virgil through the eternal realms, and Iqbal was led by the great Anatolian Sufi master and poet Maualana Rumi through these realms. In 'JuJu,' I had Sri Rama Onedaruth (John Coltrane), the Afrikan American spiritual/musical master, lead me back through the ancestral/eternal realms to ancient Kemet (Egypt), classical and traditional Afrika, my spiritual and historical heritage. Unfortunately, I feel it necessary to add that this had/has nothing whatsoever to do with the vision, goals, or traditions of white North American literature!

"Some notes on the poem 'O Lord of Light!':

Uraeus. A representation of the sacred asp on the headdress of Kemetic (Egyptian) rulers symbolizing sovereignty.

Kamites. From Kamit or Kemet (meaning the Black Land). The Kamites were the black *people* of the Black Land.

Ra. Ancient Kemetic (Egyptian) for Almighty God, whose sacred symbol was the sun, as the Light of the Universe.

Shango. West Afrikan, Yoruba orisha symbolizing kingship, whose sacred presence was embodied in thunder and lightning bolts.

Tehuti (Thoth, Greek). The Kemetic neter who symbolized knowledge, ancient wisdom, mystery, measurement of the heavens, phases of the moon.

Isis (Auset, Greek). The Nile Valley Civilization's Great Mother, 'Queen of Heaven,' 'Throne of Kemet,' the queen and co-ruler with king Asar (Osiris, Greek). Humanity's archetypal Black Madonna.

Larry Neal, Henry 'Ankh' Dumas. Two outstanding Afrikan American visionary epic poets, leaders in the 1960s Black Arts cultural era.

Obelisk (Greek). A monolithic, four-sided Egyptian pillar which tapers into a pyramid, symbolic of pharaonic authority.

Bennu (Kemetic). The original divine bird which served as archetype for the later Greek bird, the phoenix.

Orishas. Divine Beings of the West Afrikan Yorubas, paralleling the Kemetic neters and the Christian/Hebrew/Muslim angels."

DEREK WALCOTT has published many books of poetry—including *Collected Poems 1948–1984* and *Omeros*—and more than thirty plays. His long list of awards includes fellowships from the Rockefeller Foundation, the Ingram Merrill Foundation, the Guggenheim Foundation, and the MacArthur Foundation, as well as the Nobel Prize for literature.

BARRY WALLENSTEIN is the author of four collections of poetry: *Beast Is a Wolf with Brown Fire, Roller Coaster Kid, Love and Crush,* and *The Short Life of the Five Minute Dancer.* His poetry has appeared in more than fifty journals in the United States and abroad, in such places as *Nation, Centennial Review, American Poetry Review,* and *OSTI-NATO* (a jazz/poetry magazine published in London). He has made two recordings of his poetry with such musicians as Cecil McBee, Stanley Cowell, Charles Tyler, Jeremy Steig, Bill Chelf, and Jeff Meyer. He teaches literature and creative writing at the City University of New York and is also an editor of the journal *American Book Review.*

"I started writing in the 1960s in New York City, partially inspired by readings in the Village, and the coffee-house scene. I found myself, by accident one night, reading poetry with Charles Mingus playing in the background. Years later and to this day I aim for the music to be in the foreground; for the poetry and music to be one. At the end of the decade I met the singer, song-writer Tim Hardin. His phrasing and musicality surprised me and then greatly influenced my writing. The music of Charles Tyler and his responsiveness to my poetry led to a ten-year working relationship. David Rosenthal, poet, translator, jazz critic, helped me understand that jazz poems need not be about jazz artists or even the world of jazz—they just need to have the music."

BELLE WARING is the author of *Refuge,* which won the 1989 AWP Award in Poetry and the 1991 Washington Prize, and which was cited by *Publishers Weekly* as one of the best books of 1990. Waring has received fellowships from the National Endowment for the Arts, the D.C. Commission on the Arts, and the Fine Arts Work Center in Provincetown. She is Writer-in-Residence at Children's National Medical Center in Washington, D.C.

"My mother had a beautiful voice, and I grew up hearing her sing and play jazz records. For a time she lived two blocks from the One Step Down, a small club in Washington, D.C. That's where my poem is set.

"I put Monk in the poem because I like his title 'Misterioso'—a bilingual play on words. To me his composition sounds antic and canny and odd-child witty, all of which cuts against the neurasthenia of the speaker. But, of course, you can't hear the tune in the poem; all you have of it is title. A form of shorthand for emotional climate and social milieu, the title suggests that the characters are cool (like Monk) but at risk (also like Monk). (I am referring to his breakdown, which, although you could quite understandably object to how it was handled, nevertheless seems to have happened.) I put 'Misterioso' in the poem because to invoke Monk, even in this glancing way, is to summon his ambiguous juju—a charm against madness, death; a charm most familiar with death. It isn't gratuitous. The stakes are too high for that.

"A working definition of jazz poetics would include improvisation, but the discovery method of composition isn't limited to jazz types. Anyway, between music and poetry the parallels are hardly exact. The soloist plays over a beat established by the drummer; a contemporary poet writes variations on meters established by balladeers and Renaissance types. But drummer and soloist play together, while, in free verse, a classical meter may linger only as prosodic memory. The pause in a singer's phrase resembles a line break, a caesura or a tonal shift, but a page can't vibrate like the voice box.

"Still, a poetic line inspired by jazz has its own internal logic. You break it where you *hear* the break. When you see a line break that's stark, against the breath, or ornery and vivacious, between *syllables,* even—and you say, 'What was that!?'—maybe *that* is a way to give back a bit of what print took away, to lean on sound, cut it on an angle. Not to make nonsense for the hell of it, but rather to surprise the word. Surprise you too. Think of the way Betty Carter comes in on a certain syllable and holds it, playing with time. You want your lines to be like that.

"Jazz teaches the virtues of immediacy, intelligence, and sound-that-is-seductive-of-itself. Hearing jazz, you witness the creation. You want your poems to be like that."

WEATHERLY (born Thomas Elias Weatherly) is the author of *Maumau American Cantos, Thumbprint,* and *Climate/Stream.* He is also co-editor, with Ted Wilentz, of the anthology *Natural Process.*

"'never muted heart' is the melody or theme improvised in the *jazz* solo, 'times':

> never muted heart
> never muted heart
> eclectic blues guitar."

RON WELBURN teaches American literature at the University of Massachusetts–Amherst. He is part Native American (mostly Tsalagi) and part African American, "and Berwyn in Chester County, Pennsylvania," he writes, "is my home town." He has composed, arranged, and performed music. His collections include *Peripheries, Heartland,* and *Council Decisions.* In 1981, while oral historian at the Rutgers-Newark Institute of Jazz Studies, he produced a radio program on Native Americans in jazz and blues; and in 1992 he was honored to be among the two hundred Native American writers at the Returning the Gift festival at the University of Oklahoma. "Bones and Drums," dedicated to the late and former Lionel Hampton drummer Lewis McMillan, is in his yet-unpublished collection, *Coming through Smoke and the Dreaming.*

"I grew up in a southeastern Pennsylvania family of storytellers, Native American and black mix-bloods, who shaped my ear, my interest in wildlife and history, and who taught by example the significance of dry incisive humor and the ironical in seeing things long-range. Many voices have lived in my poems, including an occasionally reluctant urban one that has appreciated the pull of a city. My love for music runs the gamut of jazz to classical to pow wow and stomp dance and many more. Perhaps ultimately, my poetics honors the vision I call forth to deal with life's paradoxes, to honor six and seven generations of family histories, and the lifelong knowledge of thousands of years in America that sent me here."

MILLER WILLIAMS is the author of twenty-six books, including a history of American railroads (with James Alan McPherson), critical works on John Ciardi and John Crowe Ransom, translations from the Spanish of Nicanor Parra and from the Romanesco of Giuseppe Belli, college textbooks in poetry (including *How Does a Poem*

Mean? with John Ciardi), and several volumes of his own poems, including *Living on the Surface: New and Selected Poems, Adjusting to the Light*, and *Points of Departure*. He has also released on LP and cassette *Poems of Miller Williams*, and he is the subject of a book of critical essays titled *Miller Williams and the Poetry of the Particular*. He has received a great number of national and international awards and honors, including the Amy Lowell Award in Poetry presented by Harvard University and a fellowship from the American Academy in Rome. He is director of the University of Arkansas Press and University Professor of English and Foreign Languages at the University of Arkansas.

Instead of a prose statement, Miller Williams sent his poem "Logos," which he said was "too long to serve as my statement on jazz and poetry, but that's exactly what it is." "Many years ago," he added in his biographical statement, he "played an old Albert system clarinet in a jazz combo."

DAVID WOJAHN has published four books of poetry: *Icehouse Lights* (winner of the Yale Series of Younger Poets Award and the William Carlos Williams Book Award of the Poetry Society of America), *Glassworks, Mystery Train*, and *Late Empire*. He is co-editor, with Jack Myers, of *A Profile of Twentieth Century American Poetry*. He currently teaches at Vermont College and Indiana University.

BARON WORMSER is the author of *The White Words, Good Trembling*, and *Atoms, Soul Music, and Other Poems*.

JAY WRIGHT's books of poetry include *The Selected Poems of Jay Wright* and *Boleros*.

YEVGENY YEVTUSHENKO has published many books of poetry in Russian and more than twenty in English, including *The Collected Poems: 1952–1990*. He has also written and directed plays and films.

AL YOUNG is the author of many books of poetry, novels, and personal memoirs. His poetry books include *The Blues Don't Change: New and Selected Poems* and *Heaven: Collected Poems 1956–1990*. His numerous awards include National Endowment for the Arts, Fulbright, and Guggenheim fellowships.

"Music—with which poetry remains eternally intimate—seems a dead ringer, as it were, for life itself. And while each also seems invisible, I always catch myself asking: What is life but spirit; spirit-thought made hearable, seeable, smellable, touchable, and delectable?

"Who hasn't sung or listened deeply to songs, re-lived recordings, or melted into some performance to the point of identifying almost irretrievably not only with the sound and inner look and feel of music, but with all of its inexplicable beauty, the rapture; the crazy, life-quickening sense of it?

"Jackie McLean once told Pacifica's Art Saro in a late 1980s interview, 'Man, if we wanna sound like airplanes on there . . . we can be an airplane, man.' McLean was recalling his longtime soul-pal trumpeter Lee ('The Sidewinder') Morgan's reluctance to parachute into musical terrain he hadn't even surveyed before, much less explored. With trombonist-composer Grachan Moncur III, they were rehearsing

Moncur's modal, eerie-sounding 'Air Raid' for the historic early 1960s Blue Note album, *Evolution*.

"'So,' McLean is supposed to have said to Morgan, his longtime soul-buddy, 'let's be an airplane, you know. 'Cause Grachan is different, man. He like Frankenstein and Donald Duck and a wide variety of topics, weird topics to write music to.'

"As Mary Shelley's 1817 horror story and Walt Disney's cartoons have inspired movies, costumes, whole philosophies and music, so music routinely provides poets with 'a wide variety of topics, weird topics.'

"Like jazz players and all the other artists and poets, I want to fly, to sail, to jump and leap and jaywalk; I want to walk, skate, surf, skateboard or ski across barriers. If I play Gene Ammons's 'Canadian Sunset' and Thelonious Monk's 'Carolina Moon' back to back, I can imagine how an escaped slave must have felt once she actually reached Toronto or Montreal. How powerfully odd it must have felt to look back at herself, plotting this break; back there outside Raleigh or Charlotte, where the passing thought of Canada was a dream.

"I want to zoom forward and at the same time watch it all rush past me through the porthole blue of some cloud-blown sky-ship. Or, backlit, seated at the window of a train, Duke Ellington's favorite composing site, I have no trouble seeing and hearing centuries whiz past.

"Einstein had it pegged: the mover isn't always necessarily moved by all this movement. Grounded in stillness, rooted in silence, all motion, like sound, seems hopelessly yet deliciously relative. Even so, the beauty of all these scheduled and improvised arrivals and departures neither fades nor reaches any point that even remotely resembles a fully orchestrated stop.

"Like the advancing hands of a clock closely watched, the action we know as music or poetry will sometimes appear to stand still. But in truth it is only the quiver and shimmer of being profoundly for-real and alive that slows; the sweet, hot solo jam of believing what you hear just plays and thickens and builds.

"After fifty years of listening, I still feel as though I can't get started; as though I have so little to say about jazz and the roles all music continue to play in that curtainless sun-room in the mansion of my life, where writing and thinking take bloom."

PAUL ZIMMER is the author of many volumes of poetry, including *The Great Bird of Love, Family Reunion: Selected and New Poems*, and *Big Blue Train*. He is currently the director of the University of Iowa Press.

"'But Bird' came out of the two most momentous episodes of my young manhood. I had revered Charlie Parker from first hearing his sounds on old Jazz at the Philharmonic records. I mail-ordered more of his 78s to Canton, Ohio, from a New York record outlet—and nobody there really knew that I was the hippest kid in town.

"I had just turned twenty when I was drafted into the army. It was a brutal, totally disconcerting time, especially when the army decided to assign me to participate as a witness to the atomic bomb tests in Nevada in 1955. By then I felt so hopelessly alone and afraid, I didn't believe in anything. But the army assigned me to three months' training near New York City before sending me to the test grounds. The poem tells how I learned how to get to 52d Street. It was the end of 'the era' and close to the end of Bird's life, so I could not believe my great good fortune when I found him playing one of his very last gigs on the street. It is documented—he was having a kind of window of clarity and he was playing splendidly. Listening to him and watching him play, I could not believe the stories I had heard about him. I took these moments with me to the test ground and remembered them through some terrifying events at that place. Jazz/Bird sustained me, indeed, became something I could believe in, in the face of that ultimate evil."

Music Appendix

Robert Johnson
    David Wojahn, "John Berryman Listening to Robert Johnson's 'King of the Delta Blues,' January 1972"
Elvin Jones
    David Henderson, "Elvin Jones Gretsch Freak"
Booker Little
    Rick Madigan, "Stereo Time with Booker Little"
Charles Mingus
    Paul Beatty, "Sitting on Other People's Cars"
    William Matthews, "Mingus at the Showplace"
Hank Mobley
    Cornelius Eady, "Hank Mobley's"
Thelonious Monk
    Diane di Prima, "Notes on the Art of Memory"
    Dave Etter, "Monk's Dream"
    Dave Etter, "Stuffy Turkey"
    Dave Etter, "Well You Needn't"
    Michael S. Harper, "Bandstand"
    Michael McClure, "For Monk"
    Haki Madhubuti, "Knocking Donkey Fleas off a Poet from the Southside of Chi"
    David Meltzer, "17:II:82"
    Charles Simic, "Crepuscule with Nellie"
    Belle Waring, "Refuge at the One Step Down"
Wes Montgomery
    Mari Evans, "Boss Communication"
    Useni Eugene Perkins, "Boss Guitar"
Lee Morgan
    David Henderson, "Lee Morgan"
Charlie Parker
    Baron James Ashanti, "Just Another Gig"
    Arthur Brown, "The Assassination of Charlie Parker"
    Stanley Crouch, "Up on the Spoon"
    Joy Harjo, "Bird"
    Lynda Hull, "Ornithology"
    Richard Jackson, "Shadows"
    Lorenzo Thomas, "Historiography"
    Paul Zimmer, "But Bird"
Art Pepper
    Edward Hirsch, "Art Pepper"
    David Meltzer, "18:VI:82"
Bud Powell
    Al Young, "Dance of the Infidels"
Mongo Santamaría
    Martín Espada, "Shaking Hands with Mongo"
    Martín Espada, "Dándole la mano a Mongo"

Woody Shaw
    Michael Castro, "Blew It"
Nina Simone
    Nikki Giovanni, "The Genie in the Jar"
    Lance Jeffers, "Nina Simone"
Bessie Smith
    Alvin Aubert, "Bessie"
    Alvin Aubert, "Bessie Smith's Funeral"
    Houston A. Baker, Jr., "Of Walter White's Father in the Rain"
    John Berryman, "Dream Song 68"
Sun Ra
    David Jauss, "After the End of the World"
    Askia Muhammad Touré, "O Lord of Light! A Mystic Sage Returns to Realms of Eternity!"
Cecil Taylor
    Thulani N. Davis, "C.T. at the Five Spot"
    Thulani N. Davis, "C.T.'s Variation"
    Diane di Prima, "I Ching"
    Ntozake Shange, "Elegance in the Extreme"
Jack Teagarden
    James McKean, "After Listening to Jack Teagarden . . ."
Ben Webster
    Ron Welburn, "Ben Webster: 'Did You Call Her Today?'"
Junior Wells
    Sandra McPherson, "The Ability to Make a Face Like a Spider While Singing Blues: Junior Wells"
    Sandra McPherson, "Some Metaphysics of Junior Wells"
    Sandra McPherson, "Suspension: Junior Wells on a Small Stage in a Converted Barn"
Lester Young
    Al Young, "Lester Leaps In"
    Paul Zimmer, "Sitting with Lester Young"

BLUES (GENERAL)

Houston A. Baker, Jr., "Tobacco Warehouse Blues"
Gwendolyn Brooks, "Queen of the Blues"
Gwendolyn Brooks, "The Sundays of Satin-Legs Smith"
Jane Cooper, "Wanda's Blues"
Henry Dumas, "Concentration Camp Blues"
James A. Emanuel, "Get Up, Blues"
Mwatabu Okantah, "Southern Road"
Raymond R. Patterson, "Hopping Toad Blues"
Raymond R. Patterson, "Sundown Blues"
Dudley Randall, "Langston Blues"
Derek Walcott, "Blues"

Barry Wallenstein, "Blues 1"
Barry Wallenstein, "Blues 2"
Weatherly, "Mud Water Shango"
Weatherly, "Times"

REFERENCES TO SEVERAL JAZZ ARTISTS

Gwendolyn Brooks, "The Third Sermon on the Warpland"
Christopher Buckley, "Nostalgia"
Christopher Buckley, "Playing for Time"
Thulani N. Davis, "Rogue & Jar: 4/27/77"
Sascha Feinstein, "Christmas Eve"
Allison Joseph, "My Father's Heroes"
Michael Longley, "Words for Jazz Perhaps"
Kenneth May, "Valentine's Day"
Larry Neal, "Don't Say Goodbye to the Pork-Pie Hat"
Useni Eugene Perkins, "Jazz Poem"
Eugene B. Redmond, "Distance"
Ron Welburn, "Bones and Drums"

MEDITATIONS ON JAZZ (GENERAL)

Karen Chase, "What You Can't See"
Hart Crane, "For the Marriage of Faustus and Helen"
e. e. cummings, "[god pity me whom(god distinctly has)]"
James Cushing, "Autumn Leaves"
James Cushing, "Every Time We Say Goodbye"
James Cushing, "Lover Man"
Frank Marshall Davis, "Jazz Band"
Henry Dumas, "Listen to the Sound of My Horn"
Cornelius Eady, "Jazz Dancer"
Anselm Hollo, "Le Jazz Hot"
T. R. Hummer, "Poem in the Shape of a Saxophone"
June Jordan, "October 23, 1983"
Vachel Lindsay, "The Jazz of This Hotel"
Thomas Lux, "Night above the Town"
Naomi Long Madgett, "Plea for My Heart's Sake"
Thomas McGrath, "Jazz at the Intergalactic Nightclub"
Conrad Kent Rivers, "Underground"
Muriel Rukeyser, "Homage to Literature"
Baron Wormser, "It's A Party (1959)"
Yevgeny Yevtushenko, "Saints of Jazz"

ANONYMOUS OR RELATIVELY UNKNOWN JAZZ MUSICIANS

Ai, "The Man with the Saxophone"
Martín Espada, "Majeski Plays the Saxophone"

Sean Harvey, "The Mighty Tropicale Orchestra"
DuBose Heyward, "Jasbo Brown"
Richard Hugo, "My Buddy"
Lance Jeffers, "How High the Moon"
Derek Walcott, "The Glory Trumpeter"

Acknowledgments

The quoted passages in the preface first appeared in *Jazz Spoken Here*, edited by Wayne Enstice and Paul Ruben (Louisiana State University Press, 1992) and Paul Berliner's *Thinking in Jazz* (University of Chicago Press, 1994).

The painting on the cover is a detail from "The Ambiguities 266," by Thorpe Feidt.

Every effort has been made to trace copyright for the poems included in this anthology. We gratefully acknowledge the following permissions:

Ai. "Archangel" from *Greed* by Ai. Copyright © 1993 by Ai. Reprinted by permission of W. W. Norton and the author. "The Man with the Saxophone" from *Sin* by Ai. Copyright © 1986 by Ai. Reprinted by permission of Houghton Mifflin and the author.

Samuel Allen. "I Say, Mr. A" from *Every Round* by Samuel Allen. Copyright © 1987 by Samuel Allen. Reprinted by permission of the author.

Baron James Ashanti. "Just Another Gig" from *Nova* by Baron James Ashanti. Copyright © 1990 by Baron James Ashanti. Reprinted by permission of the author.

Alvin Aubert. "Bessie" and "Bessie Smith's Funeral" from *If Winter Come: Selected Poems 1967–1992* by Alvin Aubert. Copyright © 1994 by Alvin Aubert. Reprinted by permission of the author.

Houston A. Baker, Jr. "Tobacco Warehouse Blues" and "Of Walter White's Father in the Rain" from *Blues Journeys Home* by Houston A. Baker, Jr. Copyright © 1985 by Houston A. Baker, Jr. Reprinted by permission of the author.

Dorothy Barresi. "Venice Beach: Brief Song" from *All of the Above* by Dorothy Barresi. Copyright © 1991 by Dorothy Barresi. Used by permission of Beacon Press and the author.

Paul Beatty. "Sitting on Other People's Cars" from *Joker, Joker, Deuce* by Paul Beatty. Copyright © 1994 by Paul Beatty. Used by permission of Viking Penguin and Lowenstein Associates.

John Berryman. "Dream Song 68" from *The Dream Songs* by John Berryman. Copyright © 1969 by John Berryman. Used by permission of Farrar, Straus, Giroux, Inc., and Faber and Faber.

Gwendolyn Brooks. "Queen of the Blues," "The Sundays of Satin-Legs Smith," and "The Third Sermon on the Warpland," from *Blacks* by Gwendolyn Brooks. Copyright © 1987 by Gwendolyn Brooks. Reprinted by permission of the author.

Arthur Brown. "The Assassination of Charlie Parker" and "Callin Buddy Bolden" from *A Trumpet in the Morning* by Arthur Brown. Copyright © by Arthur Brown. Used by permission of F. Nicole Brown on behalf of the family of Arthur Brown.

Christopher Buckley. "Nostalgia" from *Last Rites* by Christopher Buckley. Copyright © 1980 by Christopher Buckley. Reprinted by permission of the author.

243